Where The Horse Takes Wing

WHERE THE HORSE TAKES WING
I GO ALONG·RIDING
THE SHADOW SIDE SADDLE
TO THE NEXT SPRING· Madeline DeFrees

Where The Horse Takes Wing

The Uncollected Poems
of Madeline DeFrees

Edited by Anne McDuffie

Two Sylvias Press

Two Sylvias Press
PO Box 1524
Kingston, WA 98346
twosylviaspress@gmail.com

Cover Artist: Nancy Canyon, *Palouse Sky*, 2016 (acrylic on paper)
Frontispiece Artist: Hui-Ming Wang, from the series *Small is Not Little*, 1978 (woodcut)
Cover Design: Kelli Russell Agodon
Book Design: Annette Spaulding-Convy
Photo of Madeline DeFrees (back cover): Rosanne Olson
Photo of Madeline DeFrees (interior): uncredited
Photo of Anne McDuffie: Rosanne Olson

Created with the belief that great writing is good for the world, Two Sylvias Press mixes modern technology, classic style, and literary intellect with an eco-friendly heart. We draw our inspiration from the poetic literary talent of Sylvia Plath and the editorial business sense of Sylvia Beach. We are an independent press dedicated to publishing the exceptional voices of writers.

For more information about Two Sylvias Press please visit: www.twosylviaspress.com

First Edition. Created in the United States of America.

ISBN: 978-1-948767-03-3

Two Sylvias Press
www.twosylviaspress.com

Praise for *Where the Horse Takes Wing*

Where the Horse Takes Wing, Madeline DeFrees' uncollected poems, published in her centennial year, afford a reader the unique opportunity to follow the arc of a poet's vision for sixty of her ninety-six years, from the convent to the university, to her beloved garden. Madeline was world wise, and that wisdom infuses these poems. "Everything that moves, loves and is afraid," she once wrote, and in a single line one recognizes her deep compassion for all creation. That said, she was also discerning and pragmatic—with a sense of humor. One sees it pointedly in her closing poem, "Pre-Need Planning": "Caught up in details: bills for burning my bones/and delivering ashes. Cost of an urn/ for the ashes and a place to keep them – I lament this long distance dying. Why must I choose/memorial music when the melody //in my ear is Today?" Her life and her poems were both spiritual and spirited, and in that way her work provides a blueprint for the examined life. She is a role model for poets, and we are grateful to her literary executor and editor, Anne McDuffie, for so carefully assembling and making Madeline DeFrees' work available for the world.

—Sandra Alcosser

ဆ

From first poem to last, DeFrees reminds us that she is the master of craft: rhythm and sound composing a music which lends her poems a lasting reverberation. This thoughtful collection, compiled by McDuffie with loving patience, reveals once again DeFrees' wide range of subject and form, enflamed in her later years by passion. Clear-headed and straightforward, many poems shine with her kindness, kindness which shone on me as a beginning poet when she helped me believe in my poems enough to move forward, to keep writing. As this collection demonstrates, she followed her own advice, taking wing with her usual aplomb and flair.

—Alice Derry

ဆ

These as-yet-uncollected poems and fragments, left to us by Madeline DeFrees, have lit up my world like morning sunrise—as Madeline herself so often did. Let's bless her for these great-hearted gifts.

—William Kittredge

&

Reading this beautifully edited book of Madeline Defrees' uncollected poems is like seeing a flock of rare and ruddy birds set free. The poems hold the vigor and courage of a poet speaking up from the shadows, from her double lives, from wind, water and body. As DeFrees herself has written, this is a voice that had "stopped looking / for [her] own likeness or the echoing names of what [she'd] learned in crossing" and "Suddenly we veered into sun."

—Frances McCue

&

For Madeline DeFrees, her early cloistered life did not deprive her of experience but intensified her instinct for ordinary moments sprung from silence into poems of revelation. As she said on leaving the order, a willow tree is rooted, but this does not stop storms from making it wild in dance. So she brought fierce sensation and fearless insight to the page, where "the truest real / is the real that cannot be seen." In these uncollected poems from her long career of lyric devotion, her prismatic attention storms our own lives.

—Kim Stafford

&

The poems of Madeline DeFrees are, like their author, very seriously playful. They have always been that way, as you will see when you read these previously uncollected ones. Of course she loved language; all poets do. But you get the sense, when you come across a passage like "swallows skate in razor turns / across the floodlit afternoons," that the language loved her right back, just as seriously, playfully, and beautifully.

—Robert Wrigley

Table of Contents

II: Body of Wind and Water

III: The Dream of Double Life

Early Work

Introduction

The Widening Stream

I arrived at the University of Massachusetts, Amherst, in 1982—the year Madeline DeFrees' *Magpie on the Gallows* was published. I was surprised, along with the other poets accepted into the MFA program, to discover that both Madeline and James Tate would be gone for our entire first year! As I recall, Jim was doing a visiting writer gig at the University of Alabama, and Madeline was on a Guggenheim Fellowship in Cannon Beach, Oregon, working on a book-length poem that would become *The Light Station on Tillamook Rock*.

Needless to say, the news floated the incoming poets into a morose, self-pitying state of anxiety, presided over quite comically by Russell Edson, our guest teacher for spring semester. Edson, for all his outrageous brilliance on the page, was profoundly shy—a dapper, nervous man who was by no means comfortable leading a workshop. Instead, at the beginning of the semester, he appointed a student named Timothy to be in charge of the class. "Timothy," Russell would say, sipping from his well-fortified can of Shasta Cola, "What do *you* think of Dorothy's poem?" Timothy was the happiest person in class by quite a margin.

Naturally we were thrilled at the prospect of Madeline's return the following year. We were expectant, primed, perhaps a little worried, too. Had we made the right decision in coming to Amherst? But Madeline in the flesh more than made up for that first floating year. For me and for the other student poets, Madeline became a teacher, a mentor, and an exquisite role model for how to live a writer's life: the life of the mind and body brought to bear on the liveliest of spirits.

Each week Madeline led class with a co-conspirator's zeal. She understood our poems and what we might yet accomplish in them better than we did ourselves. Somehow, she already believed in us, divined the potential in our inchoate soundings, and assumed we were all as smart and sparkling as she was, up to poetry's imperatives. "No otherwhere exists—"

> for sound, sense, spelling,
> fitness, savor on the tongue, and all the pointy
> oddments of mosaic from which a word, a phrase,
> a language may be pieced.

"Gloss on a Line from Mallarme"

Delighted by complications of sonority, idea and image, she nonetheless had a sniper's aim for anything done lazily, carelessly. Madeline was an editor's editor, just as she was a writer's writer. "You like to list in threes," she told me while critiquing my thesis (and cooking me a lovely zucchini au gratin dinner in the bargain). "Every list in your poems has three elements. You're going to have to watch that. And make sure that you run your eye down the left margin of your poem to see that you don't start every line with the same part of speech; you're fond of doing that, too."

For all of Madeline's devotion to the rigors of the craft, she was, at heart, what any true artist is—a passionate subversive. A dismantler of expectations. She had no style bias you could count on or handicap, no "po-biz" agenda she wished to carve into Parnassian fame, no faintheartedness before the new or experimental. She wasn't interested in cultivating disciples; she had no dynastic aspirations other than passing on her belief that writing poetry was the most pleasurable, the most unpredictably revealing and sustaining of pursuits. Madeline invited us to be daring, and to revel in the mystery inherent in all great poems—what Jane Hirshfield describes as poetry's simultaneous impulse to hide *and* seek.

Here then, in a six-decade span of previously uncollected poems, is Madeline DeFrees' bold but enigmatic claim for individual female identity, undiminished by even the strictest circumstances of her early life as a Roman Catholic nun. The poems of *Where the Horse Takes Wing*—written between 1949 and 2009—are unapologetically *of the world*. They do not attempt to flatter God or woo readers. In poem after poem, Madeline inhabits her female speaker's experience with radical authority and elegantly restless syntax. Her strong authorial presence, like her clear-eyed mysticism, bears a practical relationship with the natural world.

Unstop the voice in the green earth
under leaf-mold limp with snow
and heap a remembrance fire
to winds that were in the towns below.

What dies again came back
counted or told in stone
and weight lies easier in the dark…

"Raking Leaves"

In his 1978 foreword to DeFrees' *When Sky Lets Go*, Richard Howard muses about the unwrapping, the *coming out*, so to speak, of this former nun "casting off the habit." He observes a tension in her poems between the woman once "chastened…into habitual service," and the free woman who now "has made herself intimate with us without making herself less private, public without making herself known." Indeed, there *is* something beautifully, simultaneously unbound and private in the poems of *Where the Horse Takes Wing*. It distinguishes Madeline's work from the brash "strip tease" of ur-confessionalists Sylvia Plath and Anne Sexton, but also from the fabulist work of the male poets she'd once had so much in common with—Deep Image poets of the working-class American landscape like Richard Hugo, Theodore Roethke, and James Wright, and the cooler, more cerebral stylists Richard Howard and Howard Nemerov. Certainly it distinguishes her from the wave of neo-confessionalists of the 1980s and 90s such as Sharon Olds. Like Jean Valentine, Franz Wright, Anne Carson, and May Swenson (to name just a few), Madeline DeFrees is a gestural poet, a nuanced conjuror of mood and fleeting moments experienced in the surreality of everyday life. As such, she uses her own past as tenor and vehicle, not as destination.

When the project is discovery—true, unplottable discovery—there is no percentage in exploiting the facts of a lost and heaven-bartered youth. Adept at hiding and seeking, Madeline DeFrees' poetic persona in *Where the Horse Takes Wing* is whip-smart, wounded, bemused, ecstatic, arch, world-wary and wonder-struck by rapid turns. She does not romanticize earthly suffering or use it to bargain for old-school eternity. Neither is she the star of her poems, only a member of the assembled party. And because she is no ingénue, regret, too, plays its part. In "Safari" (1994), the speaker mourns a "story lost in / Seams so deep and still that one can barely hear / The trickle in the fossil water."

In a sense, Madeline's speaker *chooses* to find herself lost midway on the journey of her life. She understands the risks and knows that such a journey is perilous because it is essential.

> I gulp the bracing air
> knowing what kiss of life compels me,
> what independent means.

"The Dream of Double Life"

Having committed herself to unknown and unsentimental ends, Madeline writes toward uncanny illumination and transient grace:

> I lift slow
> petals to light. Curve to the crescent wave,
> the seed-filled urn.
> Leave by the eye's gate
> shut, by the ear's earnest window, to ford
> the widening stream...

"The Rider"

Ultimately, I would argue that Madeline DeFrees' genius, her sleight of hand in revealing and withholding, is feminist at its very core. Not because she spent nearly four decades living communally, bound to the will of others as Sister Mary Gilbert, but because she understood that a great many women live bound to the will of others as wives, daughters, mothers, sisters, and co-workers: pragmatic shape-shifters, all. Madeline makes no fetish of her particular past, but writes outward from it, enacting and recording the "widening stream" of women's shared experience.

> She flies as seasoned fliers do—by the seat
> of their sense, the dark
> cold day the instruments disagree. Wherever there be
>
> Dragons, her borders
> shift to take them in.

"The Medieval Cartographer"

For Madeline DeFrees' devoted readers as well as those new to her work, the publication of *Where the Horse Takes Wing* is cause for celebration. Reading her work across sixty years, it is impossible to reduce her to a single autobiographical note. Her life-long commitment to writing poems of female identity in complex, protean states of becoming continues to astonish, and it surely places her among the best and the bravest poets of her generation.

Dorothy Barresi
September 1, 2018

Where the horse takes wing
I go along, riding
the shadow side-saddle
to the next spring.

(1979)

I

The Way Back

Three Poems from "A Catch of Summer"

I

Half a league from Custer Drive
in a cabin 10 x 12 on a corner of the old Fort
the poet takes a stand. One blue and one green candle
below two high-screened rectangles in the double brick wall
keep the dark from being total.

EXPLOSIVES: NO SMOKING warns the sign
by the heavy metal door and the patterned wooden door inside
says how far the firing line has retreated
behind the pine-brushed peace of a summer afternoon.

The cabin turns its back
on the highway and the railroad track.

Unlocked through intervals of armistice
the doors swung to. Driven by wind or dark he stumbled in
to find a troop of tumbleweed taller than any fear
and twice as volatile: an arsenal of deprivation carried to
infinity. And winter on the way.

He did the ordinary things by day: no sudden gusty word
to sweep the hordes from cover; never a careless match;
none but invited guests; and for the rest,
a padlock, sturdy, to divide the In from Out.

You see him there, framed in illusions of the open door,
lock in his pocket, hand upon the key
declaring his final war.

Aggressors with brooms, trespassers on private dooms
he sends astray: through anthill, skunk hollow,
up unreliable stairs; into the tidy jungle
or the tangle of years, while he waits
patient as any mole, for the dark to disappear.

II

Sundown.
And the Great Northern Crane
comes whooping through the valley
where I train my eyes to take their cedar
poled beside flatcars of butterfly-yellow
cats crawling to the wormwood farms.
I feel the cold compartment
of the Western Fruit Express
in its too green wrapper cut low by evening
nuzzling the Cushion Ride, and guess
the terminus of all those trussed-up dreams,
technicolor Henry Fords, engineered
towards extinction by an orange diesel
and hordes of coal-black coal cars.

Fluting through the unmined night
I carry the burden of the railed rejoinder,
crouching with my kind in the crumpled
echoes of a cry on wheels
and deliver the almost men.

III

After the whirlpool flowers
caught in bright buckets of song,
after the shaken summer
and berries dark on the tongue;
after the final burning leaf
and before it goes out in snow
we walk through our private distances
into a no-season you will not find
on any calendar because the ear
has never heard its name.

I drop a small stone into the well
of your loneliness and watch the ripples
widen where the still sky
drowns in your silences. Fallen
or struck, the morning floats
at our feet and though we do
not pick the strayed
mock-orange we remember, it hangs
on the air like a forgotten
number or the first fall.

In clump and thicket, tree trunk, burrow,
yard, the wild things sleep
kept by the house they guard. The collie
fleeced and warm, playing dead
on the fog-chilled ground, abandons
any dream of skunk or flying
needles for the chipmunk frozen
on logs, that scolds and entertains
and plugs every hole with the essence
of pine till the cold blows over.

Let them all live, the dog
says in his sleep. And we do,
no longer afraid of our shadows
on the ant-embossed stair
to the echoing wood, knowing
how sheer the winter lies
on the pitch of a roof engineered
for explosives, now beamed
toward the tunnels of light—like the poet
who pondered the summer and won.

(1965)

In the Scales

(From "A Catch of Summer")

I

July dust covers the ever-
greens where I lie, heavy
with summer, lost in the opaque cry
of the owl drowned in day. Or wake
to the nightly blare of the great
horned moon and the grave sinking
of stars. There in the full hour
I go to meet my time and gauge
the drop from a ledge of light into
sleep. The hand rounds on my shoulder,
ticks in my finger ends, follows
the slow blood to the crack in the wall
till I knock on the dull disposition
of bodies, casting the weather
of all that weight and, deliberate,
turn my face to the fall.

II

At halfpast summer when the creek
bed runs dry downhill and the
rolling stone outwits the law
to shed its gravity every
thing turns to straw:

foxtail grass that took the sun in
chase, green in the turning light or
red, disheveled and whiskery now;
toadflax sprawling and spurred
to the finish; tumbleweed

skirt over head, blowzy and blown;
the best gone to seed, pressed in a pod;
on hollow stalks dead or in husks
mocked up, their powdery charm sifted
like butterflies racked.

And bachelor buttons stuck
with their sense of form
through a colorless time.

(1966)

Postscript to "A Catch of Summer"

The cabin stands. Explosive as before.
Its padlock jimmied from the listless door
dangles a strangled neck to let me in:
the murdered mind returns to haunt a scene.
I match my foot against a dusty track
and beg for miracles to bring the child back.
Though spider curtains part, the threshold coils
with headline rattlers painted there for miles:
murky green and witches' blue
where open-eyed cornflowers grew.
Small skeletons of birdsong heap
the heavy skies excluding sleep.
Lupine that fell like saving water
snaps its jaws, an alligator
in purple mazes cheating lost
adventurers of lovely ghosts,
and yellow flares explode in grass
grown three years wilder than it was.
My shallow footprints stain the rain-wrecked stair
that floated by me all last winter
and swallows skate in razor turns
across the floodlit afternoons.
The cackle of the weeds gone dry
wails perennial revery.
Bordered by false forget-me-nots
the hollow grave says bodies rot,
and absence echoes more of thieves
than resurrection of the leaves.

O death to whom all bright things come,
honor the coin of your kingdom.

(1968)

Stalactites

What grows where rivers rush
into concavities beyond our search
and drop, their stunned streams veining out,
incised in rock and hushed before they fall;
what grows is largely lost
like dreams across the temporal.
Away from sun the unguessed music
and the known return of night upon itself
breed flowers of a strange and stern conception:
pale yellow, brown, icicle-spiked,
the copper-blue and lurid green
we know by touch or magic.
Magnified by enclosure in gardens out of time
they draw us like love into the dark,
hollow earth, the gradual brilliance:
the downward thrust of crystal
into an underworld.

(1965)

Ballerina

Poised on one toe in snow
she will not let it hide
the only thing that saves her:
the grace to bear that bareness
by all those evergreens.
Wearing her knots and scars,
she leans away from the cliff
to stiffen her faith in rivers.
Her limbs bend back to let the wind
reform them. Crooked for keeps
she leaps the gap and pirouettes
from habit to show how practice
balances extremes in acrobats
and dancers.

(1965)

In Plato's Cave

They were all there chained in air
over the rockfast waters
off Anacortes, heading for the islands
that will not be submerged
whatever maps we go by
on the ever green State Ferry:

that figure on the foredeck, older
than Ahab or Noah, pipe
and jutting jaw below a glance so keen
it cuts a swath before the prow has time to;
matrons in slacks, backs
to the intricate rigging; couples young

for centuries, profiles tilting at love;
and the shadows variously bound
that live by images recorded
on the brain of a single lens
reflex. I watched the trim
seaman's legs down

the precise stair from nothing
to nowhere and stopped looking
for my own likeness or the echoing names
of what I'd learned in crossing.
Suddenly we veered into sun. The shadows
broke for cover: smoked glasses, cabin,

or the deeper shade of sternmost privacies.
Struck awake by the grim light I remembered
seeing it all before
when a bird's wings blinked across a high
window to decorate the dark
wall of my prayer.

(1965)

Waiting for Proofs

Once or twice a year the blood
of martyred Januarius, brought near
the relic of his head is said
to liquefy, informing the closed vessel
with a pulse to thaw the centuries—
miraculous!—or merely accidental—
according to where you stand.

I honor miracles myself but keep
an urn at hand, containing what
is most my own: blood, tears, sweat, bone
and that decisive breath that makes
the difference we know as death.

I wonder. Entombed in your antiseptic pages
will the blood quicken to confound the ages?
Or will a cold curse hold off the sun:
Here lie the pale relics of a nun.

(1965)

Rehearsal for a Reading at Reed

Rehearse. Middle English from Old French: *to harrow again.*
The harrowing of hell. That is to say, the just delivered
by Triumphant Christ out of the lion's jaw, the inexhaustible pit.
Caged by the thought of it, I read in chapel and cloister,
on buses and city streets, in bed and on my way to class;
read to beards and braids and uncombed hair;
the erudite and the arrogant; atheist, existentialist, Beatle and Beat.
And always to the unorthodox, intellectual elite,
I read...read...read...in my square, Roman Catholic
convent-bred, conventional voice, terrified by inter-
rogation, inquisition reversed, indifference with a difference, and the
sophisticated rehearsed regularity of question and contention for which
I have no answer and no defense nor any hope of finding
either. I am harried and harrowed again; buried alive in an oh-
so-elegant coffin: in short, re-hearsed.

At other times, I stand up tall in my flat shoes,
my vision narrowed by the strict white gauze; my voice
disciplined by a salutary pause, and pipe in my reed-
iest tone...songs of no consequence on dull
themes—my own—that are certain to register as religion
or repression, delivered, they will surely say, in Gregorian
chant. I remember my formal indiscretions and will not recant. Though my
sons be in the furrows, I will not turn them under
nor sulk in my private tent to save a tender heel.
Inexorably, my rhythms march in steel columns,
each stolen gun leveled at its own dark head
as the ancient cry rends the torn throat, stretches
the muscles tight and falls on autumn air to the banked
flowers by the bare creek bed sown with dissembled bone
and flanked at the crossing with gilt memorials to a broken reed.

(1965)

Turnpike

Somewhere in New Jersey the Joyce
Kilmer Rest Stop flags
travelers in summer wear miles
away from a solitary tree though this
is hearsay and the poppies may be
blowing in rows over that dead
prospect which I know only
by a dust cloud of tourists settling
one hundred odd miles from Hoboken.

When you told me of this your eyes were blue
as the house and world you live in
or the rain of robin's eggs I
walk through. Together we paused
in the shade of a lovely irony knowing
how little the journey has to do
with rest; why heads of state stuff
platitudes in hungry mouths
to please little old ladies
who haunt legislators; and why
the flowers brighten always
over the wild, lost grave.

(1966)

En Route

Past lava rock and sleepless fences,
late winter-grazing cows
and the sage of eastern Washington in a grey-
hound leap of unadorned precision,
a stage before the sun, for economy...
for pleasure and for poetry in just measure
I journey to Moses Lake with my operator, T. E. Dell.

While the coach is in motion I do not talk
to the driver, inaccessible over the white
line I must stand behind. Farm
machines like artillery rise early to guard
the Ritzville Warehouse and Obie's
flashing home-made pies where the
OK Rubber Welders splat
grain elevators to flat skies as we cruise past.

In one lurch of unaccustomed gears
near the Last Gospel Mission—
Christ our Creed, Love our Law—
we search the dead-end diamond yellow
warnings and do not turn.
A Carnation truck, funereal, looms
through the fog and water slides thin
and clear under the cracked ice of a wayside ditch.

Cigar-smoking and coveralled a foreman
watches us by, then signals
his earth-moving alter ego
high in the cab to get going
and straiten those levelled mountains—Twenty-
two Deathless Days Parking
Elks Only—for our motorized ride.

(1966)

My Wilderness is Seldom Absolute

I've found impressions of a slippered foot,

Mistaken them for mine and turned to see
the circling steps repeated endlessly:

havoc diffuse as the hurricane
railed and delivered like a first-class train;

all the dark things that night can tell
shrunk to the compass of a human skull;

bloodroot, dogbane and foxglove dried
with Latin labels and a pharmacy guide;

potions and charms to contain the will
as casual as overkill.

(1966)

Tranquilized

No worries, thank you, Doctor,
except that my head, too dahlia-
red and dangling on its airy
stem remembers no more music.

I eat well, sleep three meals a day,
blot up the sunshine
on the garden path during my constitutional
and after my daily bath,
rub down and warm up and relax
with your marvelous pills.

I have got rid of fever and of chills
and keep a ninety-eight-point-six
the way some people keep
Commandments.

What if the morning ticks
to parentheses at dusk
and after I do not smoke
I sit in an overstuffed chair
and leaf through a colorful non-book
that taxes my eyes
as little as my untroubled mind?

Yes, the neighbors and even the family
have been unusually kind
and nobody says a word or seems
to notice and certainly not to care
about the oversized crop
of wilted lettuce replacing
my fallen hair.

(1966)

Gloss on a Line from Mallarmé

Well then, if the poet's be the charge to purify
the dialect of the tribe, let him not stand mute
and spectate while the villains lop
the rounding syllables from fore and aft to rarefy
or carve them up to suit their barbary taste.
Let him, as valiant Caesar says, look to't
and not truncize the bloody corse or pare
magniloquence to merely big. Such butcherage
would not be beauteable among sequacious men—
a kind of English usury the impecuniful
can never tolerize—though, god of suffixes
be praised, we still apostrophize
the aftermath however poisonful.
The words I would retire are younger, true,
less beautious by an ell, less brilliant possibly
than Chaucer's (one who Chauces) might translate.
If what the masses say can slay a form,
deprive a root of sap and flower; make its final hour
a happy hunting ground for academic excavationists,
I say, Poets of the World, arise!
Revive the word so dastardly interred!
No otherwhere exists—for sound, sense, spelling,
fitness, savor on the tongue, and all the pointy
oddments of mosaic from which a word, a phrase,
a language may be pieced, a truer adjective, archaic,
obsolete, standard, colloquial, and eke
for poets meant, who ought to struggle some
before they give consent that dictionary dolts
with bumblebolts ruin the Sleeping Beauty, Ugglesome.

(1966)

Raking Leaves

Unstop the voice in the green earth
under leaf-mold limp with snow
and heap a remembrance fire
to winds that were in the towns below.

What dies again came back
counted or told in stone
and weight lies easier in the dark
of a sinking April moon.
The crush of last year's apples
stains the track
where leaves hang flowers
on the branching smoke,
veined with the primitive light,
stirred from their beds
to blacken singly in the starlost night,
their ashes falling
on our granite heads.

(1967)

The Real Canary Islands

The bird coned to the end of that huge
Christmas pine stares past my childhood
like a moulting parrot that will not talk
whether to swear or beg for crackers.
Unwilling to let go he nestles into a screen
of electric needles greener than mould
or envy, to withhold any word I can tame
or fondle. Always I am afraid
that the bird will break in an ornamental
shower too bright to pick up; or come alive
in a volley of dung burning me blind.
So far away that I cannot see them
unnamed birds push red skiffs
into purple waters and sail into sounds
too deep to follow. Only the paired flash
low over waving grass in a gold whirl
of never was, tells me that the crow's signal
is not all, and the dumb parrot is a liar.

(1968)

The Least Romantic

The bartender gags on Keats. Hears elephants
trumpet in the coffee urn. Screek of wind
through screen reminds him of some crow
out of his past, making the scene. Good shot.
He burns out his wiring several times a day.
Never could stand giveaways. This man divorces
what he loves. Tromps on decoration with quality boots
remade to fit his standards when industry fails.
His eye has stops to catch the weakest light—too much—
develop images like fossil prints that carry
weight to keep the spirit lean. At 38
"a child in the ancient light of the sun,"
he calls himself an existentialist,
drives his car like death three years farther on.
The only way to go for a pro. Behind the student's
eyeballs, window, shutter, Cyrano and Zorba
interrogate the stranger. Nudes warm the walls.
An annotated copy of his favorite naturalist
rests against a beer or brandy.
The darkroom here lets in what light he chooses.
Calendar and clock choke on schedule,
the bed waits for the monumental sack-out.
And the telephone, the unwritten poem, rings on and on.

(1969)

The Most Authoritative Desk Dictionary Ever Published

does not list *ombudsman*, an official appointed to receive
and redress grievances against the government.
That book is too authoritative to believe.
How can I credit a public defender
with an unlisted number or define a role
by the obvious hole its absence makes
in the fabric of justice? If I could redress
the grievances I'd dress them all in boldface caps
with mix-and-match diacritical hypertribes drumming against
the desk, the dictionary, the publisher, and the
crooked little scholars who had the whole thing rigged.
It's too alphabetical for words! Between *omber*
(the 17th century game of cards with a stacked deck)
and that city in Sudan, *Omdurman*
(a desert if there ever was one) some primitive chieftain
or Occidental woodsman has rubbed out the

                                 Ombudsman.

(1970)

On the Rim

In the grass, a dark shape that will not purr
or hiss or sing its name, buried in fur,
in skin, in feathers and deep grass. After a while
the chipmunk stops flagging its tail and blends
into the branch in a cradled trance, limp stripe
dangling over the limb like a twig and bright eyes
big with stupor or sleep. I wait with him,
wanting to warn the victim by throwing a pebble
or stepping on dry grass, but cannot move.
Sunflowers chide me with wide brown eyes
where I sit, neutral ally of magpie or cat.

"Don't," I scream, but the word, like a dream-
word cannot get past my lips, and my knees
dissolve in a tender breeze. The pine rocks
its small bundle and tips it awake.
I watch the chipmunk mobilize lax muscles
and head vertically towards the noiseless place
in the grass where flowers fold him away.

Often in the night I wake to the shrill
chip and rattle of the kill—some cry
or ambiguous leap announcing the end
of everything, including sleep, but the waiting
goes on, and the silence.

(1970)

The Way Back

The way back was blocked. In a roadbed overgrown
with spiked grass and wild roses, some trespassing
was called for. Today I dug up the whole
damned park and planted it farther west
where the dry season rocks the Pacific
off the Oregon coast, and evergreens come up fir.
In the pines' asymmetrical shade, a green bird
flashes me back to a weedy lot. Grasshoppers
spit tobacco juice into my open hand.
Behind a wooded screen some far-off
engine stalls, and butterflies, common as cabbage,
flower the stalks. Fog, cool at my throat,
muffles my voice, and moss says
Never mind the cracks. A light weed
in blond sun dares the wind to strike
it white overnight or bald, but nothing comes
of all this except the nodding twilight and slow peace.

(1971)

Judging A Poetry Contest

At ten o'clock on Tuesday morning I cannot tell
whether a crippled elephant is better
than a bat with a bleep in his radar.
I keep five reasons why I still exist
on my bedside table with a grocery list.

I am looking for a leopard with stripes so wide
they knock the eyes right out of your glasses,
but here, instead, are the authorized spots.
These messages were not written. They rolled
from regulation desks in tidy dens while the cub
scout master made like a bear at the office.
Or they stenciled themselves on snow of remote peaks
glimpsed by Sunday drivers in seat belts
of a winterized Buick.

I want suicide notes
scribbled in lipstick on Kleenex. Once a year, some cheap
Valentine monkey business for the janitor who has to
separate the garbage from the beer bottles on Monday
and throw away everything that does not
say unmistakably: *I am a diamond*. A man
with a toothache and fallen arches does not
need to be told where they are.

(1971)

Our Man in Mindinao Reports on The Tasaday

I

Deep in the rain forest the Tasaday had never
seen the moon or known the astronauts who mapped
its craters. They passed their Stone-Age lives
by jungle waters eating tadpoles, baiting
monkey traps with wild bananas. They have no word
for iron, run from the big word thunder.
When rain comes on, as in this photograph
they huddle under palm fronds, cut them
for umbrellas. The floor of their forest home
(They build no permanent dwellings), tangled
fern, rattan, vines, ground orchids.
Robert Fox, a Panamin official, helped them
make a clearing. They had seen the sun
but did not know who owned it.

II

They do not have, they do not have: rice, corn, salt,
radios, contact with the sea, agriculture,
aquaculture, sugar, pottery. They do not have guns.
Snakes frighten the Tasaday. One of their gods
is bingbang. Their word for *think* is *dum-dum*.
They forage for wild vegetables. The deeper you dig,
they say, the better the fruit. The most beautiful thing
in the forest is finding choice wild roots. They may be
the only people alive who do not know tobacco.

III

Defal, a neighboring tribesman, bird who walks
the forest like the wind, found them, the lost tribe,
these gentle people. Years passed, a few. He brought along
one or two others, told authorities. It is all so startling
to them, like lightning, as they watch the giant bird
descend, the head of the Presidential Arm emerge
for National Minorities. Enemy is just a stranger's
word. Notice how shyly they put bare arms around
the savior. Where do you get all those things you carry?

IV

Their shallow streams flow clear, musical as their
language—wild pigs and *sela dang*, dear to them
in season. The tribal name their fathers dreamed
could double for a mountain. This mug shot of a young man
drinking from *talungtung* is all bamboo and water.
On slopes outside, brush-burning neighbors open land
for farms. Cold wind bites the clearing. The drone
of Elizalde's helicopter, loud on logging roads
disturbs the timid eardrum. The Stone-Age hearts
of Tasaday, who have no leader, consent he may be god.
When forest yams give out, will he invent potatoes?
Now, this talk of reservations, people to protect.
Next month Fox will lead a band of scientists deep into
their secrets. He gives an old man sugar cubes,
headache pills, tells newsmen Tasaday are healthy,
do not want to leave the forest for good. The situation
is complex tonight. Natives file their teeth
by satellite and the sponsor's message comes on.

(1972)

In the District

This morning the Open Door Clinic is bolted and barred,
shades over its eyes, tiles blue in the face.
Down the block a cripple bangs his crutch on the lock
of the Hoover Appliance Sale and screams into
the vacuum. The Liquor Store's corked up till noon.

I pass by wild sweet peas between huge rocks,
their seedy guarantees hung over asphalt curbs.
Blond's Barber Shop, shut to all but information
and emergencies, leaves a number on the glass.
I want to know what length of beard, sideburn alarm,
seduction of soft curls would ring the bland proprietor
and bring him in.

    On campus, my compass is a dome.
              The oxide spire of the church, nearer home, goes
  off like a rocket, its
mumble of mourners inside: "Pray for
my son...deserting his country." I pray for my lost country,
past the driving school that specializes in nervous cases,
damp coming up through cold institutional floors.

At odds with racks of genteel china, Oriental trays,
rugs that slip and slide, I keep a chain
across my door, housebroken mirrors trained to catch
my lies coming and going. A face to crack at every knob
I turn. And mould threading its secret life
through the rye bread in my larder.

(1972)

Sunday Service

For Richard Hugo

You liked the plain wood cross that lonely rain
and weather marked, no Latin on the road to Carbonado
and the dead cement stair to a blackened tavern.
We took the road together in the Sunday air.
Your woman in the doorway who disappeared
inside was really me. I tried to let you know
the water black around old hooks
and lures, Kapowsin's lake of cedar stumps.

We drowned the vulgar paint in wild mint, forgot
the flaked-out crowns of burning saviors, bass
along the bottom with cold eyes fastened wide.
The wine I chose grew warmer in sun you couldn't
share. I gave you Coke instead, a sunburned ear,
the wine to Fred, counted how often the woman's
name you tried could make your mouth soften
though smoke and opaque glasses let you hide.

You said the blonde barmaid in the new Kapowsin
who worked insurance with your aunt would look
OK, if she kept herself up. Fred brought the book
you signed. She served bitter coffee with his beer.
I caught her mother's glare, drained the cup.
They asked what your poem meant. I heard your last
words cross the lonely bar like wine. Like water.
Not bitter. I knew the rites were over, let myself go.

(1972)

Capistrano

It was the pigeons clapping their wings in sun
I could not celebrate.
The note they cooed grew fat
on government grain in rocky alcoves
where they stared sightseers down
and in the square
perched on housewife humps
of women moulting in their middle years.
Down corridors so lately underground I made my way
by air currents.

Past the tallow pit
the brick lined hole for tanning hides
the numbered stations of a tourist ritual.
What happened was my own affair:
the entrance fee
insured against no losses.
Walls were wattled clay, floors
eroded brick,
skies flapped white above us to light
reluctant shoulders,
break into beaks at our feet.

Everywhere the signs admonished me
to feed the poor
who fed the pigeons. They were legion.
I closed the tall church door,
knelt on brick before the gold
high altar shipped from Barcelona—the beam
in my line of vision
an original older than the garden. Around me
milled my brothers and their keepers.
I signed my forehead with the cross,
darted by the well-fed flock
promised to skim home lean with the swallows.

(1972)

A Regular Deposit to Your Savings Account

I've read the signs. Lived too long by glib
directives, broken lines stenciled to my skull,
the body's weight swung desperate from a tree.
The light show I swallow once a year
goes home sad with headache.
Don't tell me happiness is to save it.

To trespass when the field is wild with flowers
feeds the great horned toad, the spiny anteater.
Risk is its own reward. Sweetness
in the head, light breaking through veins.
My version reads: Feed anything that isn't dead.
Taxidermy is the greatest crime.

Time to shift the label from the teller.
Before carpets, splinters stood for shock.
We reach for light. A static crack suggests
we ground all feeling. That blank check
makes us fold into ourselves, bankrupt
lives given over to the safety cache.

(1973)

Trepang Fishing in Webster Creek

You wade into wide water at low tide,
net spread for the catch that is always there.
A suicide off Egg Rock or kettle of mutilated
fins planted by the Fish and Game. Asleep,
you heard lines of night crawlers in refrigerated
hatches, sprawled cold as spaghetti over mounds
of lettuce, the sea spade ringing like a clam shovel,
where bubbles break and go down in stiff air
off Crown Point. Remember how you stood on that huge
stump over the backed-up Pacific, shadow-face eaten
by ten-footed crabs. Rake's pull and underwater sun's
toward the child you held down till the lungs
filled. Rank hair streams through kelp beds.
Minnow eyes dart through holes in the rock face,
hands close like pincers on lost parts of yourself.
Narcissus in an inkwell. After the drowned small lives
with their watery limits, not quite vegetable, you come
to the sea-cucumber in Webster Creek, transplanted
from the South Pacific to this inland stream like
Chinese soup invented to keep from starving.
You devour whole recipe books, gaunt as a nanny.
Later, slow-moving claws boil red in huge waterpots
on wood stoves. The tender meat. Mounds
of cracked shells, their bodies towed away
at the owner's expense. Soil and sand raked over
a bony prominence. If you look both ways
before crossing you will eat tomorrow.

(1973)

II

Body of Wind and Water

Found Poem: Goat Island

Four hooves left no tracks on the ice bridge
near Great Falls. On that backward island looking west
the white goat broke her tether, sidestepped
ambitious boys, the ways of weather and captors
of her kind. Duck and crane did not intrude
on her essential work. Alone, she chewed
what had been swallowed, purebred contemplative.

I see her now, that even-toed tough mammal,
cousin to camel, deer, giraffe. Lighter
than sheep, wary of fenced-in plots. Her complex
stomach fat with rejects. Let me claim
again the symbiotic goat who helped me
claim the world, hard-headed, when cow's
and mother's milk, all formulas, were poison.

Here in the family album, cold as reason,
her sire's backward curling horns cannot outdo
my father's peasant pride. He owned the hungers
he survived. Rude stock, my squall, worse luck
of Mother's orphan fears. He farmed them out on Sundays,
kept books all week, the record straight, figures
neat as milky monuments on cemetery plots.

Old Goat, don't give up. Chew on your close-cropped
island. I move to give you back the whole wild state.
Glacier, Flathead Lake. The limestone caves near Whitehall.
Domestication is a sad mistake. Three forks
conspire to keep your land surrounded. Outwit
them all, your only company the migratory birds who
reclaimed the island when other goats were gone.

(1973)

~ 37 ~

Beating the System

This is a toast to one of those
double loaf towns. Walla Walla,
perhaps. Or West Falls, West
Virginia. Wherever, on the best
maps, there's a small power source
and a factory for plastic clips:
little loving traps to engage
the necks of wrappers we buy
bread in. Snowflakes are never
identical twins, says a drift
of evidence. Under the hungry
lens, glow of cool cheek,
blue-shadowed brow, renew the stale
eye, leave the beholder weak.

In a seizure of plastic confetti,
a breadline of breathless days,
Washington Jones, cog in the cosmic
machine, punched out bread wrapper
closings with soul. Regal as cigar
bands they circled the product
they'd married. Clamped off air
with a heart-shaped kiss. Under
the mechanized code and color
concessions for the gross,
Jones honored the personal rhythms
that kept them unique. His
accurate fingers re-ordered
the jaws of that uniform bite.

Cold under a drizzle of plastic
stars, the town walks with closed
eyes through his white fall, eats
bread alone, and lives on the odd
shapes that guaranteed it fresh.

(1973)

Woman with Coiled Braids

They blamed a horse for the scar we could only guess
at night small and shaking,
trying in our beds
to part those lengths of hair
and peer into her secret.

In our dry hours the shining green of oaks
declared the woman safe
who knew that far sweet rumors
slept their tides
through spirals at each ear.

Silk came to a rippling end when she unbound it.
We saw her huntress-robed
to net the moon,
the snare blown back
to show her perfect body.

The disc fell heavy as a hoof on pillowed clouds
her head supported.
We watched the crater fill
with the nightly grief of that wavering image
at the bottom of the well.

Nothing we understood would lift her streaming hair
our vision kissed awake.
The ghost came back
to swing from gloomy braids in the very tree
where sun had played our games.

A noose around the throat of strangled leaves
pale bones tossed up
on beaches of the sky. Kelp trailed the kite
we dreamed frail as paper
the ribboned sunlight bounced again.

(1975)

Moving

Pried from its wooden stand
on the middle of the block
our two-story house on Oak moved slower
than my watch
through white summer days to its vacant lot,
a neighborhood of early mowers
on Siesta Drive.

My sister arrived dressed for the second shift.
A cool beauty at eight she knew about
things coming apart on sight.
Hands over my ears
I heard expansion joints wrench,
stared faithful as a god into that crater.
The furnace looked silly
barely able to keep itself going.

Bedtime was better than that.
In the moonflowing street
I eased into
those hollow rooms
where headlights swept the shades, asleep
all night in the sweet hum
of the traffic.

As feeling affects the body,
as a sleeping mountain moves men,
as Shasta Daylight transports honey in tank cars,
that old house moves us again.
At the Office for Short-Lived Phenomena everyone says
contact the center of volcanoes
if you want news.

(1975)

The Social Register in Hillsboro, Oregon

When the saxophonist married the mortician's daughter
our town pulled out all the stops. The band
turned Danube-blue departing from its score.
On a scaffold by the bank two workmen lost
their footing where pale carnations swung from lampposts
Mayor Blunk had dedicated to the founding fathers.
Weil's Department Store unveiled a cold surprise,
feted December brides. Severe in silken caskets
double bands of hammered gold filled Abendroth's
show window. Third cousins filed past. A five-tiered
cake appeared in Warner's Bakery with an orchestrated
wedding party frosted pink on top. Reverend Haller
practised square knots in his study over Boy Scout
meeting rooms. Stiff fingers of the organist
intoned a Lohengrin. Four singing Nolans sent
sophrano trills from houses honey-colored by the moon.
Florists tended bleeding hearts and straight
sweet williams. The price of rice went up
two cents. Dry goods hit a hundred yards.
Elks declared a moratorium on death and the blithe
rehearsals lengthened in the anteroom.

(1975)

Reviewing Three Portraits

Two clocks out of synch watch faces of night
drift by. One face, a lacquered saint, dredged up
from a trunk, wrapped in virgin wool, black
robes of justice trapped in the vault of a bank.
An 18-karat guarantee of stainless steel and peerless
dentistry, though you'd have to pry the mouth open
to discover that. A high-priced portrait photographer
in Chicago crossed her nervous hands on a Rule Book
and said, "Don't smile!"

Steel girders support the lifted face, the smoky hair
and smoky voice exhaling clouded lines. A four-wheel
drive studio, props in every back street
and a live camera that really moved. Peeling paint,
thin pulse in the temple, faint warnings of early
snow: shadows, assurance, perspective. Nothing
has been left out of this head shot because it was not
pretty. He said, "Let your hair blow anywhere it wants
and go right on shouting your poems."

In this quick candid, everything turns grey. Impartial
light circles the hair. Something live as the nerve
of a tooth crosses the route from forehead to clavicle.
Lash and brow serene as in that common face on the silk pillow.
Soft music saying, You must not call this by its real name.
See, I have cosmetized the lid, kept the slack jaw
in line, disposed beads at throat and wrist.
It is not your time—not yet—says the paid mortician
stroking dead hands strapped in place.

(1974)

Poem in Answer to a Birthday Card with Photograph
of Cedar Waxwings

For Lee Nye

Waxwings flake the vault. Your calligraphic cry,
sharp against white sheets, blooms the rigid limbs.

Diagonals of going mutiply in a storm of crosses
dark as the lank freeze coming on. They thaw

November skies enclosing me alive, loosen a flowing
older than my bones to stretch the shrunken sun.

It tingles down the spiny currents of departure
messages of never and of now. Blown by an overload

doves fly out of my mouth looking for water,
are swallowed up in snow. They teeter on the crown

of mountain ash to drink orange berries dry
and try their charcoal wings. Your name hangs near

in a breath of birds, frees the heaven around it,
sharpens by definition the cutting edge of time.

Singular in the void, you memorize my loss. Small
winged thorns cling to your signature to lift you

out of bounds. The season mourns. Behind
arrested images, others flock: the gesturing hand

with its severed thumb, wide-angle eyes, a hawk.
My name a prey to cold blue flourishes in air,

the messages go numb. Your lean pulse trips the switch.
Thin years fly halfmast songs. In dreams I keep

rolling them on my tongue, hot lines
to hold off sleep. Wind sucks down the gorge

blizzards of darkening birds. How can they fly
so airy and fierce, fed on ruin all around?

Twenty years behind me an Indian tracks
the forest of lost cries. A pitted chief surveys

the crippled scene, stalks my greenest lies
with slim reminders of a civil tomahawk.

I have no years to hide, must carve my name
on those demented trunks. Along the lighted branch

small bodies flicker out together. Lovers kiss and die.
Come, hold your featherweight to a nest that needs it,

emptier than sky. Comfort the cold smoke
filing past and drift the floating

ash aloft like birds. Too late to stake
my body to the fire I raise these tribal chants

to the curve of a scalped moon and cool
my fevers rolling in the snow.

(1975)

Triptych

The bird nested
between archangel wings.
The wings were stone.
My devotion to fluted columns
is absolute. I stood
under live wings and dead wings
not knowing what lifted me.
There was a door lower down
with two pairs of wings
arching over it—a Latin
motto nobody troubled
to read. Something about learning
or piety or battle. The subtle
connections raised in concrete.
I felt a robin
light on my stone shoulder,
scrabble of bird feet.
A stone thought rounded
my skull. The wedged wingbeat,
small as a fledgling note.
It swelled, vaulting
the whole sky in a foreign
drone. How could anything
build from a hum that high,
boring through stone?

(1975)

For Cynthia: A Portrait

Mustard and green you wore merged with the field,
the river, some plot
behind hazel eyes in serious light
to make your hair unwind
that darkening spool. I saw its skeins
around the hanging
pool of garnet, jade and opal. Shades
of a Tiffany lamp, no imitation.

I thought how tinned escargots marinate in white
wine. Dressed in herbs and butter
they spiral back to the shell
where the cultivated palate aims a tool
to call them out. Unnatural light glows on base
metal or earth old as pebbles
in the streambed.

My sculptor friend stored urine in tins to weather
welded brass. If you believed art she said
you'd give the way clouds do without embarrassment.
Turned green, the hammered forms
fused with land and air, my favorite
blue. Not the indigo of water,
not Prussian or gunmetal. More like teal, the true
plumage of the hunted game bird.

(1976)

The Leaven

The bones knitting in the picture window
where a stalled air system
presses back the pane. The vacant woman
turns her face towards evening.
Her cheeks are loaves
readied for the oven. The household moves
under the placid windings
to a satin finish. Skilled needles,
ferment in the dark mass,
she's done with kneading. On the table
Lee Ward's crewel picture kit
with seven numbers circled.
The sulphurous hands swing by their own faces.
Sun falls from the room, its leaden round
mowed down in the valley.
Only the partial moon, ascendant,
lights the hooded figures.
What are we waiting for?

(1976)

The Rider

Weeks later I floated those hot springs,
wind in my face upturned, rain
on lids and the mountain
sulphur and water, the faint blue of a match
struck in a cover of cloud.

Disorderly roads near Cedar Run Creek
changing sides, a candle
veering in wind. Continuous rain
on Elk Meadows pasture
gutters along the soffit of rock where moss
pads the underside of the overhang.

Rain glazes the flat painting of farms
on my windshield, the horse
in low relief, an icon bearded and blown.
Colossal over the arbor gate
it hangs in zircon air, in the ear
floating. Under slant light rose hips
mix with the full moon.

Body of wind and water, I lift slow
petals to light. Curve to the crescent wave,
the seed-filled urn.
Leave by the eye's gate
shut, by the ear's earnest window, to ford
the widening stream,
riding the mouth of many waters.

(1977)

The Chow, a Dog of Ancient Origin,
Has a Blue-Black Tongue

Yet we accept her kisses, affectionate as air.
Unlike the famed baboon
who ran a railroad in Zaire, you will not find her
taking care of house and garden,
missing legs or drawing water. She's
not in the almanac, not
a working bitch.

Man's friend, the purple carp, swims up the ladder,
goes down slow—
running weedy rivers to a muddy bottom.
The dog who helped the baboon help
his master's dead. A suicide.
The red-eyed vireo with perfect pitch repeats
his note all day.

Zaire, come here. Let me pat your muzzle. Plate 45,
your map's a purple chow,
puts out a skinny leg to the Atlantic. A 20-mile coast
where blue whales dive at 20 knots
and come up spouting chow. Your name rebounds
along the track of pidgin. Hurray for the almanac!
The railroad takes care of its own.

My tongue, blue-black, licks the seams of syllables
like dead shells on a firing range.
The shell repeated bluer than the almanac, a lead charge
carried home under the heart's
old sandbag. I read that weather. The cartridge light
glances off the black-
lined mouth, the dogtooth violet.

(1977)

For Ed Harkness Lost in A Contributor's Note
   in The *Quarterly West*

Maybe you wrote too near the vanishing point
and that coyote cover serenading
the moon is your mourner. Did you trip
on a mismatched foot,
fall over the western edge mapmakers took
away into Pacific cold
like the sad mad rest of us grieving?

Ed, we know you're in there. Come clean
or we'll shoot for the moon. We follow
the faintly criminal
cast of your poems. You can't trust
these underworld types, their masks and their
patsies. We know all about your hearing
loss. Didn't Beethoven deaf hang around till 80?

I'm sorry I wrote asking for those books of mine
you didn't borrow. It's OK if you keep them.
Just make things right on the planet. Take over
the word, dead or alive. I favor
a dim religious light, myself
stoking the furnace with coffee, stalking your *eyelost*
wind with trained police dogs.

I've staked out the P.O. and the Little Mags,
tacked WANTED all over town. Ed, this is the dead
letter office in sheep's clothing,
Washington on the lam, code perfect, every page
bleeding into the gutter
waiting the new moon of the next issue.
Forget that fine chap

        book stuff. All of us love you.
Send the regular contributor's
poems. Here's 50 moons of reward.

(1977)

RSVP List: Regrets Only

Some nights I skip the party because my teeth
tusks and the polar ice cap is a crown
I wear to keep the skull intact. Look, I'm a nervous
driver. My husband, the late
pretender, spokesman for the WCTU, drives
a hard bargain down the center
lane. He leaves me chipping ice from windshields
on the old highway shoulder.

The labels I'm wearing feel mixed-up. This close
to sheep country, it's no thrill
being tagged a genuine acrylic virgin
lined with the look of lamb. Some days I can't
imagine who I am, stuck in a Gobi windstorm, riddle
of limbo, lobby of no-man's-land. Nothing you say
gets off on my floor. The shaft I'm falling
down, no metaphor hits bottom.

My gears are stuck on bad luck getting worse.
When we go over crimes they sound
rehearsed as clumsy introductions. Seymour, this is
Clare de Lune. Clara, Seymour. Surname
starts with L, rhymes with only and cover. Don't
push the emergency lever,
Lover. And note this well: whatever runs lonely
or amok, don't bring up the cage.

I want to go home and count sheep. I'm gathering
wool. When power's restored the tusk will be
ivory, three trunks full. Abandoned to its freight,
the lift climbs out of itself, ivory buttons
glowing. Ivories make the music we hum, rolling
pairs of straight seven's. Up from soft soap,
down from ivory tower to street
level, we watch our step. Passageway out on One.

(1979)

Frost Warning: Letter to Helen

It depends what you prefer: to lengthen
the salad days, outwitting weather
or stay cozy inside, letting the first cold snap
take all. I go for the crazy colors,
head mapping the chill moonshade of carrots,
beets bleeding into the ground their wounded legend.

I don't mind these blue-collar hands stained rich
as the freezer. Papery socks of onions
brought from the cellar bask in sun that reminds me.
Your hands on the garlic press—deft
flash of the knife culling the last morsel of flavor,
its acrid scent adrift in the room.

And the philodendron, lover of trees. It will
reach for them from a far corner—survivor
of nine-day thirst, gas fumes
and the scant notice of scholars.
Planted in a brass cuspidor, *spittoon*,
the word a forgotten object.

Mirror of metal, my face convex. That makes me
smile. The knitting goes on, dark blue
in the old trunk, color of longing. Enough time
for that good yarn. Last night,
putting the squash under wraps, I saw you
stuffing the kids into snowsuits.

Transplanted three late-blooming volunteers, brought them
indoors for the night.
Well, it didn't freeze. This morning,
sun splashes tomatoes a healthy red and I am glad
Matisse allowed every color
its zone of expansion.

(1980)

First-Class Relics: Letter to Dennis Finnell

I wanted to wear your name religiously for the rest
of my life, asked over and over,
spending my threepenny choices on Lucky Bites
from the general store. We understood fooling around
could be serious, the way our crippled uncles
coined arias. One day I heard bells
celebrate angels called to their given names. My plot
to ring one for you went flat, patron
beheaded by the fat music director's stubby hands.
She said we might bring luster
to that holy handle, but she wouldn't like it,
identity sunk—mud or menace—in slang.

                             It was slang
breaking out in a rush of letters I couldn't write
from the old enclosure, my mail censored. Dreams
turned out, patched comforters to air. I thought of you,
though, coughing and blinking, dipping your Sunday face
with the others. And I heard the tall
unhappy note of your voice
catwalk the trestle, drawn by the owl in your mama's
boot. We were deep in 'mad water,' all right,
flaunting that scrappy Irish kin
I tried to adopt as a child. I loved the straight
line of your mouth, uncertain French
asides sneaking out from balloon characters.

Good thing you didn't flinch when balloons rode
circus track to the old Hotel, and you went along.
Deranged pots lined your mama's stoop
and kettles, black on pink linoleum. Over the cracked
lintel, azaleas burned, twin red spots
in the pale of your face. I keep a diary of what we
learned. You were thrifty with letters, using them
more than once, a new address every week. "Is it
one or two?" I'd say, plopping them in like sugar lumps.
Two. First, last and always. Oh, you
were a deep one. I've rhymed your name with an Iowa
town ever since.

                  Once shaking off the town dust, you
headed for the Roman wine god, our letters
always crossing, mostly missing. That didn't work,
neither did you. You tried the Parisian bishop's act,
head carried in his own two hands.
Pastoral letters. You were good enough to shake
the basilica over the tomb of your betters, the green
night we met under the clown's umbrella. I knew
I had to change. We planned my tough escape by moonlight.
The day your daddy bit the bullet, I put
your name on the map. You'll find seven worn-out letters
by the date book next to the calendar of martyrs.

(1980)

Song for the Snow Shovel

Why does everyone hate
the new town crier of the white
plume? Supposed my shoulder blade a pedestal.
Shovel, a bottle rack found in the drift. Shaking
the burden from trees, digging a muffled
neighborhood for the bare
concrete: what absurd lives wait
to be discovered at the fringe.

I skim the paws
of animals let loose in first light, trail the kids
zigzagging from school. Chip the reckless
tread of cars hunched over the buried
curb. Indoors, the scrunch of my blade undoes
the love knot, returns the dreamer to the raveled
sleeve. No other watch but a hound
shut out by a sleepwalker.

Outside, it is not cozy.
Berlin Wall down the middle of the street. Great
Wall of China bounding my yard. Ice
clamps down, incisive, over the eaves. In air
too still for chimes, a yellow-tailed bird
flares toward the mountain ash. Orange berries
nest in shivered leaves. Chinese bells of a dog collar
bringing kisses to my feet.

Later, the city will
send its elaborate weight down the block. The town's
great will be out lifting the hulk of day on striped
shoulders. Reading their news by the window
thaws my hands on a mug, a purple finch
entrenched at the heart of a plum, both of us
spinning our wheels.

(1980)

Story Hour in the Motel Office

"Lo and behold, and so consequently, I was holding
my breath." He shifts his weight
to the right. He is with the Lamont Earth-Moving
Co. He has lost his '78 sales calendar
for the thirteenth cliff-hanging
recitation by rote. We wait, the complimentary
instant cooling in our hands.

        "Now I don't have
nothing against a particular race." The operator
turns his head. "...but I'd rather rent
a unit to a colored than give a Mexican a bed.
They have a particular body odor." He underlines
the need to be careful. "If there's two
words they know, it's *legal aid*."

        We hear: gerbils
in the pool, broken pairs, the pistols and pills
young ladies leave behind——each
tagged with number and name awaiting instruction.
You can't call the home of an overnight guest
who might have been cheating, though the manager
doesn't say that: "Maybe he or she happened to be
with someone who was not

        their legal partner. You'd
make the real woman mad." A man who loses
one shoe and doesn't know where, will squeak back
"before the thirty days ends
that we hold it." The manager has been holding it
all night. He sets his jaw for the voice
breaking out of the ring:

           "Sonofabitch. Had my rig
on the road since four…good money
for a room. Can't take any more of this fucking
noise." The manager's tired eyes
are going under. I dive from a height, swim
towards him from a long way off. "It is all right,"
I say, "I am the lifeguard."

(1982)

On the Caminito Venido

On the Caminito Venido by a house I have
never seen, a man feeds pecans to the squirrels.
The man is a floating dentist.
The squirrels are fat.
They crack the nuts with their teeth
under the raised flag near the watchdog
of the Caminito Venido.

Two-four-six, the number defeats
expectation ending in *nine*. I am closing the gate
of the picket fence on my first
visit. Digits of cast bronze cling to the post
of the country mailbox, making it mine.
Improbable scent of noble fir. My fingers graze
a black enamelled BOX.

I go back after dark for a check in the high
beam of my headlights. Under the awning
three figures of inlaid walnut
glued to the stucco. The fourth lies in shadow.
Asleep in the Caminito moon, squirrels dream
Venido pecans into pine nuts. The box
is tin. I lower the flag.

In a wind from the north the pampered squirrel
reads the entire winter, loving
the lie it encloses. His tail, the flagship
I follow from guarded rooms
where the squirrel chatters and John pulls teeth
from the rabbit sleeve. Maria
opens the box on my letter.

The sea blooms into San Diego and my lost brother
recedes from the Caminito
tossing all night on the shore.

(1983)

Lecture Under the Moose

The glass eyes used by taxidermists are generally too spherical.
—*Oxford English Dictionary*, "Taxidermist," December 31, 1869

Ritual brought us together under that wide
umbrella: an evening of cold cuts
and transcendental moons. All of us
stuffed in winter coats, filed
stiff-legged, past deans preserved in glass,
some taxidermal dream
of large ruminant mammals.

Over the chairs of mounting local heads—a light
snow on the window side—a pair of logger's tongs
swung perilous. Hooked by an expert
line, the framed trout churned water, went down
without glory. This was a big game story
our eyes held, the terrible
territorial gaze of bull moose.

Where now was the shy vernal lover who minced
the tender shoot, loose tongue stripping
softeyed leaves? He wore the season's rack
like a mitre. A clearing appeared in ground
the herd had trampled. Our leader
did not mind whose aegis he was under, spared
the mirror vision our eyes countered.

Whoever stuffed this head, housed eyes in glass,
chose a sphere too absolute. I write this
on a stone. Three young bucks wander
from the herd, tracking moosecalls once removed.
I follow suit, borne on a far
chinook. The antlered brow grows
wide enough to take in what's been thrown.

The moose stands on his head, lowers a hook
like the stick of a bumbershoot
the poor fish grab with tongs. We blow them
ritual kisses. Great Moose, translated
Mighty Muzzle, bemused by rhetoric
your candelabra mounts a wick for every prong.
Transported in that blaze, we speak in tongues,
tranced eyes and reckless heads
lifted off to interstellar spaces.

(1980)

III
The Dream of Double Life

The Medieval Cartographer

from her imaginary cell, plots a paper universe
before the compass
comes to pass. The East lies
still at the top margin. West—deeper down
uncivilized. No darling of the gods, she feeds
on desert locust. Over the left edge, the demonic
side, her stylus engraves a text in the wax
where land falls off from the rectangle:

                                        There Be
Dragons. She plunges into a vortex, whirlpool
of the next minute, not drawn into the deep
by the recognizable shape of monsters
hauling her under caves of enchanted sleep. Tangled
in bedclothes, in seaweed
slick to the touch, free of the pendulum
sway of the body, she is one of us, already
inscribing the word.

                        Hippocrates steered clear of
the link Darwin will miss.
She flies as seasoned fliers do—by the seat
of their sense, the dark
cold day the instruments disagree. Wherever there be
Dragons, her borders
shift to take them in. She conjures the anonymous
untamed names and faces them
down. Her map holds oceans at bay.

(1983)

The Whaling Wife Awaits the Captain's Return Home
(From "Whaling Wives")

My name is Desire. When I was sixteen, the roses
thick at my sill, I committed my heart
into the capable hands on the tiller,
married the harbor master from Marblehead, whose blood
was a match for the sea. The days
we sailed on a honeymoon, sweet clover
filled every cell. Then the river ran dry. Or rather,
merged with ocean, changed to a passion
for whaling.

       I was afraid for his weather, tides
that carried him far away
from the peachblow silk of our wedding. Four years
I've stood, moonface pressed to this window,
drawn into his flaring wake. The leaded glass
cut soft curves to a hard edge. Sky and water mixed
all together. I heard the humpback
singing near the boat, saw lanterns hang
in the rigging. I longed for a floor that did not
heave and sway.

       From the Friendly Islands, he urges
truce between me and the mistress of this house.
I remember the summer he brought me, a bride-
gift to his mother, small thanks for that. In the yard,
apple trees arched under their white
burden. His sisters ran out to greet me. In clumps
and hedges, purple lilac swelled, and the woman
who filled the doorway, stood against the light. I was
not expected. She stooped to kiss her son, turned
her back and went inside.

I am sick of instruction
in the wifely arts. When I put my ear to a seashell
the cries quicken of mutineers
strung up from the yardarm. The firebrand
torches his way to freedom ashore. Already the crew
has taken enough whalebone
to corset the dark women of Roratonga and Salababoo.
And the brothers, whose word sustains me here,
allow her full command

of this vessel. They promise
farewell kisses the day I decide to jump ship
and *will not* notice the untouched food
growing cold on my plate, the smoky taste of meal
upon meal from the hold.

(1985)

Desire Hathaway II
(From "Whaling Wives")

I set up house in a timbered cranny of the ship's
cabin, my heart already
heavy with hope and his child. I would not yield
my body to his mother for delivery and answered
his every argument with wiles.
Some visitor must have reported I wear
bloomers on deck, as is my habit. The words
hung still in air when she dispatched,
posthaste, her frosty disapproval. If she were to
guess my condition, I should have little
peace. My husband insists that she must know
very soon or be unforgivably
offended. Across the wide sea, it appears, armed
truce continues, although she cannot
touch me here.

               The crew is another matter, the men
satisfied with nothing
meaner than my husband's undivided passion. I see
my true rival is the Arctic Ocean.
That, and his mother's cold blood.
The one standing watch calls him from our bed
at each imagined peril. I do not quarrel with duty
but have been already widowed four years and would
be shut of that. When sailors jest about the easy
women of Talcahuano, his eyes
freeze over like hers. Can a son alter his nature?
I feel the small mouth pulling
at my breast and can believe *my* blood enough to warm
another's. I do not need the ship's glass to show me
clearly rough seas ahead.

(2009)

Desire Hathaway III

(From "Whaling Wives")

The island company he left me in was bland enough
to bore me: the wife of the consul.
One of those women who cluck and coo over their
strutting husbands. When I showed her
the dress I'd made for the child's birth, a devious
bit of embroidery of Nathan's ample,
untried handkerchief, she said it would not do.
We made our rounds of the shops, felt every bolt
of cloth, chose between lavender and

                                                   ivory, ivory and
summer yellow. Inquired the price as if the child
might wear this souvenir from the arrival day
forward. Such, the beginning. As time drew near
for my lying-in, she snipped,
tucked and gathered, starting over every morning,
Penelope besieged. When the true labor
came, I was alone for the first time,
my belly gripped by devils. I must have screamed
the door open on a witch's foul

                                               rags, charms, and
mumbo-jumbo. Astonished, I found myself wanting
Nathan's mother! Cold, yes, but
clean as snow at the antipodes. I remember piled
sheets, fluffed towels, laundry
boiled pristine white, the fresh good smell of a godly
household. Some wild voice out of my body
tore the air, and I saw the door
swing wide again. There stood my fine British doctor,
half his fee already gone

                        in some dark saloon, the reek
of drink still on him. I chose against my sex.
Medical science, civilization, no matter
how depraved. Soon he had taken hold. I did
his bidding, a trussed hen reduced to obedience.
My stormy labor ended as my son's
long trial began. Stale air forced a passage through
small lungs, his cry turned pain to fierce
rejoicing. Far away, Nathan
commanded his crew,

                        satisfied at having made due
arrangements for my wifely comfort. If money were
all, he had provided handsomely, and no
report of near catastrophe could persuade him
otherwise. Thus, I must be
dismissed as wayward—ungrateful even—with no defense
except caprice, no witness to
the unattended terrors of this birth.

(2009)

Submit Claiborne

(From "Whaling Wives")

Today the cooper has made a small coffin, sturdy
and delicate as scrimshaw. Yesterday I drew a black
line around Captain's entry in the ship's
log to honor our son. When Freddie was learning
to talk, we went ashore one time
after I had been seasick considerably and could not
walk. The carriage rattled up the cobbled
hill. Freddie grew thoughtful. He looked so serious
I had to smile when he asked, "Is *this*
Grandma's house?" not knowing it
just a hack.

       Another time he threw the cook's hat
overboard and yelled, "There
she breaches!" Playing zoo, he shoved a peanut
up his nose and had to be taken to
grumpy Doctor Fowler. That's done. I made a little
wreath of geranium leaves and a white
slip of handkerchief silk for the pillow. Rough water
put a hawser on last night. Today, the surface
calm. I do not approve of Sunday whaling, but they go
all the same, leave me below deck

                  to distract myself.
Soon, the crew will be cutting in, and the stench,
more than I can bear, although I must. This morning
our cockatoo ate copper and died. Nathan
could not build a wall, but he made a wide chalk mark
to keep the children safe. Stay *here*, it reminded

Laura on the *Splendid* deck, and her toes
brushed the line. Not Freddie. He crossed and crossed
again every time he thought
no one was looking.

              Worked on the Log Cabin quilt
in weak light. Too many pieces
cut from *his* cloth. That time the deckhand set a fire
among the shooks, my hands trembled
seven days. We had to save the food, so Nathan used
an ax to break open the hold. Every morsel I ate
smoke brought back the shaking. The naked black who came
aboard in the Sooloo Sea was not
so fearful. Our hens keep dying off, our cat a skeleton
or apology for one.

              Small help from my Bible. I cannot
make Freddie an angel climbing up and down
Jacob's Ladder. I see him thrown upon the tender
mercies of the deep. We had four pigs. One
drowned in hot fat. Laura found the first waterspout
this morning. She wants to keep Fred's place
at table. Just now she brought a string of pressed
flowers—black-eyed susans from our
stay in Talcahuano, Sailor's Heaven.

              Even when the ship
leaked 2500 strokes a day, we hoped to preserve
our precious cargo. The men cheered when Ladder Hill
came into view, and we limped
timely into port, rudder, keel and shoe torn away.

(1985)

Jenny Martinson Learns Semaphore

(From "Whaling Wives")

This morning the morning watch killed the Ox
the wild horny one we got in Borneo. It tasted
quite nice next to weeks of salt
as Cook prepared fresh meat for Captain's table.
Steward throwed most all
teaspoons overboard with the dishes water in one
Callous throw. We take turnabout
now. Our black Hen was not spared as she flew
leeward, very soon Eat by two large
Birds. On deck I see how everything happens
talking with the Flags. When a Brig yesterday
hove to, I pick out Answers
from a Book which we have. It looks odd some
to carry on

        Conversation miles apart. The winds
breezed up around noon and I went
below. By night time, Moon fulls then. Husband
makes out to go after a large whale
Mate's boat had dead. I am afraid to sleep—sit
think and sew. Sometime later
cutting out in my quarters, the light so weak
I catch myself dozing off
and on, get two pairs of white duck pants cut,
then stitching goosefeathers from
Cooper's Goose saved last month in a Pillow. Hear
wind think when will Jonathan wear
clothes I make tonight. How soon ago, Husband was
Right next my Elbow

                              possibly in eminent Danger. I
picture the Catcher struck by Shark
killer whale and Worse. I would Run for the Book
never mind my nightclothes. Pray strength,
swing heavy Lanterns and Say all I mean to save
my Beloved by a hair. Far away I hear
Commotion over the water's motion, the men holler
clamor exhausted back on board. On deck,
praise God, I do not expect waving Lanterns for
Flags or the Difficult book. The men are excited
hungry in their fatigue, all thankful. I am happy
forgetting my nightdress. I look up
misty over Flags. All on a sudden I remember. This
is called wig-wagging.

(2009)

Jenny Martinson, Whaling Captain's Widow, Addresses the Historical Society

(From "Whaling Wives")

If Husband had not passed to his long long Home
he could have told you everything: the room
where Napoleon breathed his last
that had a Bust of him sitting on a monument. Fido's
persevering death. The mahomet village where the boy
crossed himself on the veranda
kneeling on a mat, putting his head to the floor
very sincere over and over. The day
Husband took himself ashore in white pants hunting
the scared traitor of a mate and come back
muddy at night, bleeding in black native dress.
The eight-year-old King in his Mother's house
who never goes out before age 18
when he can suddenly. The Sultan's 20-room House
on a hill forbidden to women, seven wives, cushions
piled high and trouble

                                     with his feet. Husband could
always relate exact details: the sea-creature
not quite lobster, we put up in rum.
The Tahiti kanaka who fell down from aloft. His feet
slipped out from under him. He hit
head against the iron rail
doubled up like a log in water. The chicken soup
flavored with cockroach and tea
steeped in spider. When you consider the snake skin
where he shed it off and the nearly 300
horse-men on horses, it says how much whaling
improves you. On a blowy day, the men cutting in
for a greasy time everywhere on deck, you
reflect the almighty loves you. We sat in Chief's
hut on a mat drinking cocoanut milk

while he sent for his wives. The mat was made of
Rattan. The Hut of Bamboo. Wives

                              had on large hats.
Some had calico cloth put up on one shoulder
come down to the opposite hip. Some did not have
any. All the women wore calico skirts. Men had
a band round their waist
two inches wide. At one end of the hut sat a woman
making cloth. The other end was afire
where they cooked. Both were smoky. Farther on
natives rowed out to Ship with their hair
colored various colors white red black, holes in
their noses and ears with sticks
stuck through. Some had small teeth made up one way
or another. The last day we set sail
for New Grounds I stood on the Potato pen, waved my
pocket-chief till the island was little
less than a Whale and the smoke almost a Spout.
These people do not have Chimneys.

(1985)

The Dream of Double Life

He merely touches her elbow,
nothing more. Her face
swims for a second
towards the voice and a door
discloses the unused
suite at the rear of the house.

Her tones are cinnamon
and orange. I let them roll
across the brown expanse
between us. Honeysuckle
climbs the tall verandah
near the pool and ivy tendrils

plant their feet as if
tomorrow and tomorrow were
a rock they happened on.
Sometimes a sense of no place
floods me, and I hesitate
between the chaise longue

and the baseball diamond. Soon
I'm the one who's stepping out
of alligator shoes. I plunge
my face in rich, dark
fur, my skin discovers pleasure
in exchange of touch. One

smile for the widow courted, who
except for circumstance
might be my double, and I choose
again against the too
expensive feet, the sable
collar, in favor of my ordinary

jeans. And when I shake my head
and come up like a diver whose lost
nerve briefly drowns, my face
averted, I gulp the bracing air
knowing what kiss of life compels me,
what independent means.

(1985)

English Teachers' Convention for The Sixties

For Dorothy Barresi

We are beating a very dead horse. Fine
lines on the lens of the speaker
may harbor a spider. Sun gives back rain-
bows from water in the web—teardrop or dew.
Amazed by the nun with the most
flamboyant credentials, we discover our own
black-and-white and a lone blue
Immaculate Heart. We're here to observe
peerless women carried away by
metaphor. I applaud the mind, the smart
Ivy-League cut of her sentences,
deplore the slightly-crossed watery eyes
in their shatter-proof shield.

Midway in a critical pronouncement, the unlucky
poem, meant to go naked
arrives in the old clothes of an emperor.
Speculation overtakes thought,
the race turned abstract as a classic
Roman chariot—hypothetical students
flogging their horses in the crowded amphi-
theater—we in the bleachers, shouting them
on as they hurtle by, exceeding our past
incredible records, and the speaker insists:
We must step aside. This
is the victory teachers are made for, better
than John the Baptist's.

Sidelined in Seattle, I sit with the spider
in your poem: *tiny unlit*
chandelier——a figure I admire more than
the spider itself, here
where they hang, sized for the Versailles
Palace. Pleased that they complicate
corners, I'm not taking them lightly——in or
out of the poem, though prose is
a horse of a different color. I renounce
the green word of envy, confess
I sprayed poison last week, a measure more
extreme than pentameter. This morning,
back in the race and running, I cheered.

(1987)

Standing in for William Stafford

Desert and English teachers went on forever, and
Bill not there to think hard for
the herd of us. I forget where we met—Pasco
perhaps—one of the Tri-Cities that
should have tried harder. Wherever it was it was
nowhere: a chunk of neutral turf
near the bomb-testing site for a ritual read to
each other. My flight—I'm sure of this—touched
down in Walla Walla.

                  Grey English skies and Grey
Elliot English in a Land Rover, come to
chauffer me to the meeting. I was in the city
all day and part of the next, an ill-at-ease lit
instructor over cocktails
representing far places in a story that could be
true. Day two after lunch, Grey said, "It is
the time you think. Let's catch a plane."
He'd given his kids

                the car keys. But where were
the kids? We yelled ourselves loony
looking behind missing trees, the spines of dead
cactuses, wondered what God used for eyes before
we came. Not quite in the nick, we
recovered the loot, beat the heck out of there.
All the way to Walla Walla, sweet
onions shiver their skins as we barrel past. We
pray for a late flight.

Our prayers are answered.
The answer is *No*. Three minutes shy of
the airport, the plane lifts off the tarmac. No
place to go but the bus station. Good
news! We're on time for the Spokane bus. Leaves
in five or six hours. "What would
Bill Stafford do?" I asked myself, and I did it:
spent eternity in the terminal thinking
for Berky.

Wrote ten or twelve poems. Memorized
schedules for Wichita and Topeka. Called
the farm on the Great Plains, paced off a peace
walk. Then, because I was still me, did a slow
Tillamook burn. We hit Spokane at nine
or ten, and Spokane hit back: darkness and diesel
fumes. I took out my crowbar key,
heaved a ton of luggage from the rack, dragged it
inside, thinking of Bill's

little knapsack: clean
shirt, socks, shorts, wrapped in a light
grey sweater. By morning I sneaked into Missoula,
unlocked my car in the parking lot,
bags in the trunk and under my eyes, feeling a jot
better than worse because I could see a star in the
hills coming on. Because I'd avoided
jet lag to come home free as a frazzled understudy
for a world-famous poet.

(1991)

Phillips 66

And so am I, walker of gusty streets when rain
aspires to snow, my car at home
stalled in a warm garage because it weathers
weather even worse than its owner;
because Dean's Texaco, natural choice for a former
prof, is owned by the best mechanic,
Howdy Lord, natural choice
for the born again, and because on his own word
he likes to flirt with women.

                              On the front page
of the *Times*, convincingly human, the Green
River killer, face composed
for the only victim to survive, looks
blandly out. I look out, too, something
alert and dangerous in the blood. The city streets
that stalk me
energize, as anger charges hidden currents in
their cells. All day

                        clouds darken and lift, all day
this gift of song, the rain without
an ending. A hooded figure
huddles in a phone booth, and I steer wide beneath
my broad umbrella.

(1990)

Poppy

Petals curve to a spectral red nest
where a dark bird flares
from the bruised interior to the ragged
edge. In wing-shadowed drift
the nightlong sorrowing song
flows up to the lip and over the lip
into air as wide as the earth's deep bed.
Its brief season past, the fledgling
cry joins prodigal seed
to the purple dye on broken ground.

(1992)

Settling for Less

So we come at last to the thorn-bitten patch
on the hillclimb where we
encounter our pale selves reduced
to a face on Veronica's veil. We'd like to
step away from the vision, weekend
shoppers walking the fragile sea of the plate
glass window, ghosts among
mannequins. When we

                  surprise them undressed,
bodies bland as our faces, all passion
has guttered out. No retreat into shadows can
save us. Nor grief rouse the good intentions
we stood on their heads like next-of-kin
stored in metal tanks, who died in their beds
and now, with antifreeze in their veins,
wait to be

           resurrected. Last night's insider
trader, lured by the unexpected—fool's gold in
feverish seams—sifted overturned earth
to discover dust in the soil. Every dream grows
redundant: the panhandler
prone under his sign on the city street; tycoon
drowning in oil; the sludge in the vein
drifting towards the heart.

(1992)

Mai-Tai Music

Gazebo for a grandstand, the band plays island songs
while hotel guests sip cocktails
round the pool. The leader says, "I'd like to
introduce my husband, the founder of the band."
She curls his fist around a mike,
locks fingers with his ringed left hand. "We've been
together 30 years."

                And now he's almost blind, one
eye, opaque and squint, and one
unfocussed in a face of stone. Something's not right
about his gait. He stands or sits, awaiting
unseen signals, his look lobotomized. "This is real
good therapy for him." She pries her fingers
loose, both hands pleading

                        on the mike, and sways her
hips, perhaps reminding him to smile. The knuckles
of her right hand graze his cheek.
His face stays set. She smiles for both of them.
All I have to offer you is me... The catatonic
syllables of lyrics in his head
escape his lips as if the music were a walking stick.

Returned to morning cold, the melody dead, guests
find the sun a myth to live with
until it goes down. Only the words linger on,
drifting like snow in the head. They remember
the words when their singular lives
touch down and the hand joined to theirs in the end
is the hand of the paid provider.

(1992)

Cortège for My Sister's Husband

The truck in the passing lane flings a stone
squarely between my eyes
in driving rain: November surprise. Arms of
the windshield wiper flail
like railroad crossing signs all the way to
Seattle. I am leaving behind
the scattered ash and the widow's double bed.

Alone behind the wheel, I am comforted by old
convent prayers for a journey—aloud: *Be with us
now and on our last... to
eternity*. Kalama: a pillar of cloud shunted
aside by a moment of sun. And whose is the far
thin voice—not mine, not the radio's—intoning
the stress of *Kalama... Calamity*, the sudden

rites. Away from the family, grieving apart, I
was in the air pointed east, land of the early
sun. More than sister by marriage,
I was the one with character ties to the lost:
lust for the perfect; hair-trigger tongue;
throttlehold on control. Reading your solo
flight—the forsaken clutch—I ride the brake to

the End of Construction and the patience they
insist on thanking me for.
When they set your ashes afloat on Boiler Bay, I
was in Holyoke checking into the Holiday
Inn. Over the last grey wave
driving towards Puget Sound, a grey heaven scowls
at the drifted bone. I reach for your hand.

(1992)

Silk and Bamboo Music

Away from theatres of gong and cymbal,
ritual chimes and the ancient
gourd, the five-tone skeleton drifts back,
rises from the Sound
and the sea beyond, carried by wind
to mount the vertical
streets of Seattle.

              The figure appears,
dim form at the far edge of the Market
where dark stalls gleam
with orange and purple crates, where
tongues split into the Old World
accents, and hawkers
peddle anomalous fruits.

                In a corner
the flayed sole, cradled in ice, lies
near the small bird trussed
persuading the passerby. Contending
instruments give of their own tractable
matter: stone, earth, gourd, skin,
silk, wood, metal.

(1992)

Apartment Complex Dialogue in the Laundry Center

Retrieving forgotten coins from my Calvin Kleins—
soggy poems in the pockets—I said
with a native's pride, untangling my jeans from blue
arms of a work shirt: *Tomorrow I fly west*
with the wigeons and whistling
ducks for a taste of summer.

                         She looked up, folded
the negligee, slinky as Diamond Lil's:
But I'm from the West! A displaced person…a small
world! Wait till I tell my husband.
He was already there in the red fanfare of the plaid
flannel nightshirt, lovingly eased of its wrinkles.

But wait! She could be a soul mate in spite of our
incompatible wardrobes. *What state?*
I asked, going back to Mae's West, shoving quarters
into a dryer. I was Alison Skipworth…
Night After Night—"Goodness what
lovely diamonds!"

                   Kansas, she said through a froth
of nostalgia. *Diamonds in Kansas?* And under
my breath: *Does this laundry lady know Goodness had*
nothing to do with it?
                       Wait a minute. You asked me
what state. I said Kansas. Now what's this about
diamonds? You can't get any more
Western than Kansas.

She piled her satin and lace
with his boxer shorts in the basket. *You can't?* My
falling face, chin first, over the Spin
dial. Then what had I been doing, all day on a train
crossing Montana? For me, it's not West
unless I can see the Pacific. Nothing else counts.
Everything else is relative.

(1992)

Voices

Socrates, you heard them too, these voices
we call the curse of traditional
women. Not the Voices of Joan spurring her on,
who, being exceptional, heard exceptional
voices. Like mine, yours always said *No* but never
You can, you may, you must.

                         Socrates, how do we
learn to trust the image under the wavering
water that almost says *Maybe? She imagines
herself the object of irregular passions*, some
credible voice declares, and my flat heels
spike, my lashes curl, jet and acrylic.
He wants to take over the world,

                         and the velvet
falls away from my fist of iron. *She believes
we believe she's a poet*, and the intricate
structures fall. Socrates, that's not the worst.
On all of the odd-numbered days, I tilt towards
the brimming hemlock, walking the parallel
shore: denials gather

                    all night in my ear,
rolling down the canal to echoing bony chambers
till *No* is the roar of cattle stampeding,
of earth splitting under us: thunder and chaos
in brainpans of sky.

(1993)

The Walnut Tree on the One-Yard Line

Umbrella wide, east and west, the walnut tree
reigned over our land and the neighbor's,
letting the breeze and gravity
divide the spoils between us. Every fall
found this trio crawling the grassy border,
a line mapped on each brain—my brother's, my
sister's, and mine—clear as a
latitude to keep us
honest.

      When first light came, we scrambled
from bed to beat the squirrels
who scavenged both yards, with no concern for
boundaries. We stashed our loot
in gunny sacks, fingers stained with juice,
then spread the nuts to dry in the shell
on screens in the attic.
Sometimes an ill
wind blew good one way

                  but nobody cried *Unfair.*
We asked the tree to mediate. Look at us
there in a record year! No fence, no evil star,
just *Yes sir, yes sir, five bags full!*
And yet that must have been the day we started
to count. Next winter bowed the branches
low as the paradise tree sagged
earthward in a Solomon's-sword-of-a-storm and
split the live trunk down the middle.

(1994)

Death and Bleitz in Seattle

Assorted characters of death and blight,
Mixed ready to begin the morning right...
—Robert Frost, "Design"

Near the Bleitz Funeral Home, the bus takes a turn
for the worse in a snarl of traffic,
rehearses the bridge. I remember the low cost of
dying, now that I've joined the mortuary
society. In the next lane over a driver rolls down
the window and shouts: *Drive it or*
hang it up! I make a note of this small
act of imagination.

              On the bus, a lean young man—
blond—with one dangly earring and a snake
around his neck, so real that I can't tell for sure,
discusses the outback with a salt-and-pepper-
haired man, pepper springing thick from the tense
elastic of his baseball cap; and a tall
red-head in blue stretch shorts who, except for the
lack of an accent, could be

              Australian. Advertisers
on the air, they clearly intend to be
overheard. When the charmer
turns to address his seatmate, the head of the snake
at the back of his neck looks ready to
strike. I riffle through the memory bank for the face
of the Queen Anne rapist and draw a blank.
Reviewing my final arrangements,

                              I recall what to do
for snakebite: *Tie off, cut & suck.* Years
since my last First Aid course, but my skills equal
the perils of life in the city. The snake
wakes up to the bell. Doubt barrels through a red
light. the trio of talkers gets off
the coach. The bus lurches out of the free ride
zone to the end of the line: a full stop.

(1993)

Insomnia

Night of the full moon: between the knees
a small pillow
eases the spine. But not the pellet-roll
in the helmet skull
like a cue ball to its pocket
on the dark side of

        the brain. Over the felt—
click and ricochet—the white sphere
glints off the quicksilver
glance of the mirror. The player, silenced
in the bedside cube,
flashes the digital countdown as he
jockeys towards morning.

        Why do vague limbs
digress from the tangled skein of
forest where daylight never
breaks through? The challenger crouches
at the ready, cue in hand, by the one
door's forbidden entry where a thousand eyes
scan the eight ball.

        Shooting all night for
the coveted black, willing the eyeball's
skitter and drop.

(1994)

Into the Light

The fall these bones remember
warns from sleep
and nine mooncycle's weight
in native waters
uncoils, locks to another level,
floats towards the channel
and drops into light.

This boat, vertical and barred,
sculls by picket fences
not yet built. Past lattice-light
on yards of pale gazebos
where roses arc low
summer moons and fans of water
driven sweet against the skin.

I let the world in, unclenching
fist and eye an hour
before midnight. The season,
Fall, when flat light
oscillates against the hills
and trees burn
golden with regret.

(1994)

IV
Shadows

Romantic Period

Not marriage you said, having tried it twice
and my heart stuttered yes, no
marriage. How could a heart survive
forsaking its true axis for the orbit you
inhabit? We'd built our lives at serious cost
on opposite sides of the continent
and the most we could do was give them up
for a week

        together. Not casual sex, either,
you warned, and I nodded Never,
agreeable in my turn to rules of role
and ritual. Hadn't I sworn to veer away from
the easy word, drawn to the long
distance line? Before evasion
split your tongue, we were one
smooth act at a time.

        We still talk every
week, skirting the edge of the frozen lake,
adjusting to the bright
accents of strangers. I know how the lake
enlarges to a frozen sea,
and with diminishing care, avoid embedded
axes that would break it up
at the center.

        I do not ask after the other
woman, who may or may not be
real. I am anything but casual.

(1994)

Safari

Before you escaped to the other, she was the Dark
Continent: source of lazy rivers
Asleep in the blood. You touched them awake
And made the drowsy currents
Break on the sandy bed like an Okavango flood.
When summer rains
Fall on the Kalahari, night-

                    lilies open at dusk
And desert antelope converge on water:
Springbuck and gemsbok, dik-dik and steenbok
Paired in pools they drink from.
Goliath herons fly, and in the still lagoons,
Relic lakebeds drench with bloom
Where ranks of pale impalas

                  haunt the margins.
Into this scene, the lovers came as to a dream
Landscape, region of no run-off.
Under inconstant sand, the aquifer recharges as
Green life penetrates the thirstland
And animals return where everything leads to
Water. In wilderness distilled

                  blue wildebeest
Sprang from cover, no longer a cloud of dust
Churning orange mist, but wildlife
Feeding in trust from the tendered hand. *In 1894*
A Maritsane woman ran to greet
Her husband, back from buying sheep to stock his
Promised farm. Bolt

lightning struck the pair,
Locked in each other's arms. Had this safari
Couple flared like that
They might have forged a legend
Durable as bronze, their bones and veins alight
With what they shared,
Not dimmed to fizzle out

in slag—cinder and ash
Ash and cinder: the slender comfort of lover
Turned to friend. Across
The river lay a thorn savanna, its wide waste
Torn by calls of jackal and
Hyena. Northern birdlife:
Spurwinged geese and

blacksmith plovers come to
Grief in the wild game
Reserve, country of lion and cheetah.
Near the Great Rift Valley, they found a land of
Parallel faults, the fracture zone.
Halfway along, the path to the cave changes
Abruptly—wave

after wave of sand-dune ridges
Scored in a contest
History fails to notice. Beyond a dark green
Bay of tall papyrus, palisades of reeds
Guard the Kalahari bedrock, its story lost in
Seams so deep and still that one can barely hear
The trickle in the fossil water.

(1994)

Property Rites

Sixty years gone by and I follow the low
cyclone fence that edges
my careful backyard plot—lettuce
heads up in tomato cages—and the not-so-
careful neighbor's whose golden
retriever and litter of full-grown cats
scatter at my approach
to rifle the raspberry patch
straddling the difficult

                    steel. This morning
glory's a west-side strangler I'm
out to kill: twines around clinging vines
in a serial slaughter. Wherever a white bell
opens, I yank insinuating
tendrils from the victim and put them
in the trash. Madder red and lush, berries
wink under green
lashes of leaf and

                    cane. All night on sleep-
haunted borders, patrolling the property
line, the young owner contends with the old
dreamer she hopes to outwit
and evade on questions of yours and mine. She
raises the fence steadily higher,
poisons the flowers that grow there,
screens out the tireless
perennial wild side.

(1994)

Ghost Patrol

Footfalls shake the porch beside my
weather-beaten door. No screen
but rain and glooms the rain gives rise to.
The dark I used to trust
assails the shuttered mind.
The dead bolt will not strike. Distraction
takes the window blind. The head
my nightlight throws
against a bedroom wall troubles my rough
repose for a long interval.

(1995)

Horticulture

Anatomist Caspar Wistar (sometimes spelled
Wister, though the *Caspar* deals only in *a's*),
bequeathed his name to a pale purple plant,
equally ambivalent: *wisteria* or *wistaria*.
If you think the plant sounds wistful,
you're probably right, and *wistful* descends from
wishful, a kind of

            hope, because it implies
the prospect of life's getting better. No matter
which law rules the letter, in the *Sunset*
Western Garden Book, wisteria follows
the wishbone flower, comes on in the plural
(floribunda): *So adaptable they can be grown*
as trees, shrubs, or vines.

            From a cafeteria of
choices, I planted mine at the foot of the deck,
gave it some string to climb on. Next spring,
wistaria was stringy—long reach exceeding
fine grasp in a lunge for independent air;
preparing to flower, dandled bunches of grape-
shaped buds in clusters

            that fizzled out like
bad Roman candles. Back to the book: *Wisteria*
can be trained...as small, semi-weeping trees...
Time to ponder my 60s poem, the sorrowful
anatomies I noted in *dried lavender tears of*
wisteria, and having quoted myself,
to consult the experts.

Advice from a nursery
specialist: *Whack it in half, then whack it
again*, a stern regimen carried out with ease to
the letter. Caspar, your namesake's
heartbreak's a whisper—one-half, cheerful leaves,
one-half, semiweeping, where cascades
of next season's bloom lie wistfully sleeping.

(1995)

A Check for the Rent

All the pills in my armory cannot
reduce my head to size. They will
only thicken the shades on eyes
whose crow's feet leave thin
warnings, black, black. Morning
is the same pitch from a badly broken
cycle. Twenty miles back
I passed a girl with scars
on her eyes like moonflowers where
rats had left reminders.
The only way bait can fight back is to widen its pores.
The sound air currents make
winding through pockets confuses
the rodents. Their etiquette whines
at a lower pitch, gnaws at
sockets. This is what it costs to live
alone. Accidents occur, you send
flowers to broken bones. The hand
that lays them on the pillow countersigns
the checks. Likely as not, jaws
snap on the hand before it gets
the roses to water. The heavy head
floats on a lake of perfume and poison,
crystals falling through gouged
eyes, and lovers throwing
pennies in the fountain.

(1997)

Inmates Arrested in the Garden

For Patricia Solon

Reviewing the long frieze of our past in the cloister
garden, we huddle for clues over this paralyzed
plot where sun moons in and out.
Back there we were lilies turned tiger, saber teeth
set, learning to kill on our own. Targets were
mostly free-ranging parts of
ourselves: we tracked and
hunted them down.

                 Late morning. The bean seed
in the cell of its dark furrow
begins to raise its head, hidden in a cowl, then
freezes in place like a squirrel. Each time we come
back to witness this abject
posture, a solitude wholly earthborn lashes the monk
to the Garden Master.

                 When I wrote of my hope for
final sleep in the convent cemetery, I was
already dead two decades. You were the one who
questioned. Suspended lives on parole,
we abandon the veil, heart-shaped leaves at our feet
shedding the hood. This is reprieve: a flowering
white along the shoot, an end to the freeze,
deep roots in the clay of
the human.

(1997)

Evolution: A Self Portrait

When Bermuda was under the state of Washington,
the state of Washington was blue ocean.
   —John McPhee, *Annals of the Former World*

In the welter of blue ocean, I evolve as a true
crustacean, crab in a crevice
scuttling silent floors, attacking divers who
neglect to signal. My eyestalks
pan the current. Six pairs of jaws and foot-
jaws lock on prey, withdraw
to the cleft in the shelf,

                         the self's deep pockets.
Carrier pigeons unload on my doorstep, pouches
stuffed with fake telegrams from
loan sharks, the flotsam and jetsam of commerce.
The squid in its puddle of permanent
ink, hankering after the jet set, wants
letters of recommendation.

                      Paper in a steady fall.
Fodder for the shredder: perpetual reams of confetti.
And my friends—writers all—worse
still, readers, curious and compulsive.
I sweep the surfaces clean before they arrive.
My friends have X-ray eyes for
lines just launched

                   from the legal pad, so I hide
everything: journals, books, letters, in a littoral
secretary. Paranoid, yes, a Scorpio

liability, but the truth is: I swim in the secret,
feint when my scribbles
parachute out of the Frigidaire into my visitors'
field of vision.

        Overhead, moon snails gleam
and starfish glimmer the end of summer.
Anemones pucker lavender mouths, and I close mine.
Parting waves deliver me, carry my carapace
like the portable house of the hermit crab, over
the sheer rock face
in a parody of survival.

(2000)

Return of the Blue Nun

She comes at midnight, moon a thin wedge in
her window, when stars pulled from
old moorings, strike out against dark. She
glides the elliptical
track with the Book of the Dead pressed to
her forehead, raids the Sea of Tranquility
for cargo long since

                    pitched into the black
undertow. Serge of an outmoded
habit—disguise by the bolt—matches the ocean
surge over an undersea fault. Fabric
turns rust in the brine, turns green.
Framing the sun-starved face
white gauze corresponds

                    to the serial white
of breakers shattered on rock. Awake,
she will need a hand, if only
her own, into the lifeboat. The deep sea
recedes, robbed of its nightly prey.
She will climb aboard on a jolt of caffeine
and set her course—steady—to the shark-
shadowed cruise of another day.

(1998)

High Idle

My triggers pre-set for fight and flight
go off when a phone rings
or a dog barks in the echoing street
of the half-cocked night.

Behind me, each random, anonymous step
takes on the shape of a stalker.
A shadow falls across my path
like a deep-sea breaker

that crests and holds for a second
before it folds over its prey—the luckless
swimmer, and the tide pulls out
with its human freight as the lights
grow dim and dimmer.

(2002)

Driving to Port Townsend with Tom, My 51-Year-Old Tour Guide

In thirty years, my friend, you may understand
how the youthful vision fades.
How an elder needs more than the strip lights
of Las Vegas merely to read
the laundry guide stitched inside her shirt.
When we're cruising along at 50
and you point out the sky, I can always find it.
Sketch in, with a sharpshooter's eye, the clouds
and colors you dictate.

                         But you warn me too late
of the dark horse couple, so sleekly built
they should win the Triple Crown.
I miss them coming and going. And the buffalo herd
grazing behind your headrest.
Just give me binoculars, night-vision glasses—even
those fancy X-ray specs a wolf uses
to undress a woman.
Of course, everything's

                         out your window, so when
you say *Look at the deer!* I turn to
the left and say, *Where?*
Where? you say, *Straight ahead!* And there, all but
climbing our windshield, a small
mule deer saunters across the road as if she owns it.
Slowly she turns her head: a model
on the runway, substantial though seen
through my dark glasses, not quite face to face.

(2002)

Strategy

To keep from losing one earring,
I follow my shadow. The pseudo-
earring bounces with every step
I take. And I ride herd on
my body as well, not losing my
head to a passing stranger or
the heart on my sleeve to love,
that bold avenger.

In this way
I find peace beyond the small
losses: a tooth to an ache,
the day of the week, the changing
address of my glasses.

(2002)

Overlooking the Berkeley Pit

...every moon has its dark side...as necessary
as night...
—Edwin Dobbs, "Pennies from Hell"

Like your heart, the black heart of Butte has a hole
in it. Wide wound in the earth,
this 600-acre lake, bigger than God,
splits open the sad underside of the world. Years
ago, borne on a crow's

                 black wing, I found a home in
this landscape: the ruined dance pavilion,
fallen snow geese, a merry-go-round gone dead.
Cascades of riddled rock mask the Continental Divide.
Destroyed gardens know earthquake

                 sleeps in the fault.
Water that should give life turns bitter. The pool
rises within. Near the Tailings Pond with its
poison sludge, we wrestle it down
to utter rituals of blessing.

            Sunflower Hill
spawns a barren moon beyond tiers of waste: moon of
the necessary night. This dark rack
drives our art—your glass, my words—the shards of
everything wrecked and broken.

For Dan Hillen

(2003)

Fugue of the Fractured Ribs

I want to grow eyestalks like the lobster, the prawn;
to see from all sides so that every approach
sends a warning. I want to be sealed in a bubble
where no one can touch me,
scuttle away with the crabs on the ocean floor.

If I could be fenced in barbed wire, I'd have
fewer worries. No danger of jabs in the ribs
from a joker. I'd never be locked
in the terrible vise of the world's implacable
huggers. I'd be safe

                        from unpleasant surprise:
the ground giving way underfoot.

(2003)

Daphne Revisited

the tree that cloaks her maiden limbs is pear,
not laurel. Apollo tracks the honeyed scent
where lacquered leaves spread wide to rain
and store the glistening drops. As if by right
she blooms—sleek white—to celebrate a bridal
better than one Apollo vows to earn.

Unravished still, like Keats's Grecian urn,
she keeps her stubborn promise not to pair
with god or mortal. Holds fast the bridle
on wayward feeling. In a firm dissent,
she lifts black branches heavenward to write
her contract: steadfast refusal of Apollo's reign.

When morning breaks, pale Daphne swears to rein
her passions in, knowing that she must earn
the freedom love excludes. The ancient rite
of virgins strengthens her to pare
the cord that binds the luckless innocent
to age and power in a deadly bridal.

Tonight, if you should walk the bridle
path of Moonglow pear's affair with rain,
you'll catch at once the wood-nymph's heady scent
and bless her rootedness. Her burial urn
is living wood and flower. A golden pear
rewards the virgin huntress whose shipwright

father, the river god, approves her right
to scorn the customary bridal.
She yields her body to the fabled pear.
Why should a husband be allowed to reign
whether or not he has the grace to earn
respect for who he is? And why consent

to shattered vows that mark the god's descent
to love affairs his powers underwrite?
She fantasizes ashes in an urn:
not his, but hers, who chose her own bridle
as orchard queen in steady rain.
Her virgin limbs remind her to prepare

the bed air sweetens with the perfume of her bridal
vows: she celebrates the rite of welcome rain
and bears the golden globe we call the pear.

(2004)

Climbing the Sky Bridge stair on my way to Suzallo Library,

                I pause on the landing to admire
the *Dancer with the Flat Hat* by Sculptor
Phillip Levine. The cast bronze figure enacts his
favorite theme—the ambiguity of
balance—including his own. Work with cement and
metal is brutal. Witness two artificial
knees, a back subjected to the knife and uncounted
injuries to the hands. I tip my head
back to look up at

                the six-and-one-half-foot
figure, feel positional vertigo
return, and grip the railing to keep from
falling at the Dancer's feet. Given the weight of
the artist's materials, the incredible
feeling of lightness
means a triumph of art over matter. How better
to salvage one's grief
as body slowly turns

                stone, already tied to
a drowning spirit, than by putting a flat
hat on one's sorrow, making
the soul and its body dance in ambiguous balance?

(2006)

Bring on the Ginko Biloba

When the locator button on my cordless phone
boomerangs a signal to my ear,
I've already searched two floors looking for
my link to the real world. You'd
think that a page so imminent would tip me off,
but no. Scanning four corners, every plane
surface in sight, I teeter on the brink
of despair. The metronomic tattoo
stalks me wherever I go. Until I lift my
left palm toward my brow,

                                      surprise the lost
phone in my hand. Later, waiting for a city
bus, juggling three carry-ons, I
extract a pass from my purse and squint at
the oncoming traffic. On board I ride
three blocks before missing
the essential moneybag. Did I drop my purse?
Panic. Loud enough to make everyone
focus on the aisle. The driver slows down,
opens the door as I move

                                       forward to general
laughter, purse strapped to my back.
Let me be frank. Let me be anyone but me. I
crawl off the bus, embarrassed but
happy, head for a store to buy ginkgo biloba.

(2006)

Black Eye

When a friend turns against you, spring air
clouds over. The coward-yellow
iris, flower that never falls, folds in on
itself. You look around the living room at phantom
clutter and feel no better in your
tidy house. You long to put a tongue in every
wound. And you have

                    a black eye. The sidewalk
won your argument. You should have seen this coming
when he turned against his father
for the father's "broken promise." The young
star in the role of judge: they're a centrifuge
reversed. Everything whirls around
themselves. In medical books,

                    traumatic hyphemia
means hemorrhage in the forward chamber of the eye.
No mention of Bleeding Hearts I was ashamed to
cultivate: what gardeners classify
showiest of the species *Dicentra Spectabilis*, whose
generic name is Greek; the species, Latin
for *notable, worth seeing*. I am

                    worth seeing if
only for my black-and-blue eye. Should my injury
prove serious, the world I see today will
fade or die in time.

(2006)

E

E floats slantwise down the eye chart,
almost becomes an M before
in the pool of the vitreous
it changes to a child's way of writing.
Then, a little off center on the retina
it slides into the optic nerve upside down,
assuming at the utterly

                    last instant the guise

of a W.

(2006)

Shadows

High above the altar of St. Francis Xavier Church
in Missoula, Montana, the six-foot
crucifix rests on a short railing under a half-dome
ceiling lined with lights. This creates,
left and right, shadow crucifixions. They take me
back to the original

                scene: Christ crucified between
two thieves. The blessed Virgin, painted on the wall,
holds the Child. Lower down, a bevy
of holy devotees, haloed Jesuits, fall to their knees:
Ignatius Loyola, Xavier, of course. And three
younger men—Aloysius Gonzaga,

                      John Berchmans, and
Stanislas Kostka—models for all of us when we were
novices. At home in Seattle I hear a jackhammer across
the street rip up the silence. Someone's
removing the concrete floor of her garage. It would
take more than a pneumatic drill

                    to disengage
the worshipful gaze of these Jesuit heroes, who
remain with me still. Remotely I know
how to love the suffering Savior. This morning, as I
walk, honing lines of a poem, something
reminds me of my only letter from

                              my fiction professor.
Speaking of his summer students, he wrote: "Bless them,
there's not a one left who can
tell a hawk from a handsaw. The one who could has gone
her cruciform way." *Cruciform*:
It's my first encounter with the word, I let it
roll over my tongue again and again until a shadow of
bravado steals across my path.

(2007)

Physical Therapy

If I turn my head east towards Modigliani's
Red-Haired Woman, roll my flexed knees
west to the Chinese Evergreen,
if I flatten my trunk against Blue Tabriz
carpet and tap the memory of the kitchen
timer, I may banish the banshee who
wailed through my windpipe,

who grounded me
in Emergency. Better to emulate mules,
relaxed under the coffee table. If I *Assume
hands and knees*—and I do,
absolutely—letting the hips sag sideways
on Hold 20 seconds, what's to prevent
explosions of dust-mites

so lately blown up
on TV? When the acupuncturist
returns my call, midway through the Buttock
Stretch, I switch to the cordless phone,
tell him he's called too late. I know he's been
drinking: two weeks of green tea
steeped in china. Overhead, Brueghel's peasants

frolic in time to a metronome drumming one ear that
keeps me alert. The chandelier darkens
along the periphery. I prop one heel on a step
that is really two
city phone books. Everything slips. Balance
means more than a budget. Faithful to these
breathtaking routines, refusing the lazy impulse,

the lackadaisical stasis, maybe my luck will
come back. Maybe I'll walk into
the next full life.

(2007)

Visiting a Friend Who Has Alzheimer's

Sometimes I think of heaven, and it's so...attractive,
she says. We're in her room at the convent
care center. She knows who I am
but garbles details of our lives together. I ask her
when she was born. *April 6, 1906,* she says with no
hesitation. That would make her 91. She's 85.
I help her out of bed,

                    take her for a walk in the hall.
When we come back, she thinks this is not
her room. We call her Bernie. The sign on the door
reads Sister Bernadette Carlson. *That's incorrect,*
she says. *Not in the sense of incorrection, but of
untruth.* I say, *I'm going to write that down.* We
go in. When she sees her

                  prayerbooks, she knows
we're in the right place. All this time, the TV
shows some half-baked military
sit-com. One frame displays a split-second street
sign: Loyola. She latches on to it. I went there
to school. It's where she earned
her Ph.D. You did, too. Not true.

                   Now her memory
travels back seventy years to: *Fifteen. I remember
fifteen. Everybody learning to skate.* Time
to make my escape. I hug and kiss her,
promise to pray, make my meditative way to the front
door. Later I hear that she's
deeply agitated. A short time after that

                                          she's dead. I
travel to Spokane for the funeral service. Read
one of her poems after the homily,
recall our years as a team: two poets pledged to
reclaim that so attractive home.

(2007)

Dead Birds Driving

I've seen a lot of dead birds driving, you said
and I saw them too: the Red-Shafted
Flicker, its super-long tongue in sync with
the windshield wiper. The Common Crow, best-known
bird in rural

        America, no doubt a great driver,
seen cruising along on the shoulder where the crow
feeds on roadkills. And if you should motor in the
south tip of Texas, you'd better watch out for
dead Chacalacas driving toward the Gulf,
serene in that sulphurous

               climate. Magnificent
Frigatebird, dead, you must give up driving, your
wings too wide for a hearse, a bus, or a stretch limo.
In Seattle with the rest of us, you must battle
inflation. Your scarlet throat sac, spectacular

as an airbag, pushes you back from the steering column.
Dead or alive, *you* must not drive any more. The Ruby-
Throated Hummingbird, dead, doubles as a long-
distance driver. Aloft, its small size
defies the logistics of driving. Doesn't stop for

Day's Inn or Best Western, takes the exit near a field
of red flowers; a border of salvia
or a trumpet vine climbing the drainpipe. This
smallest of birds quenches its thirst from a beaker
made of the vine's blossom-cup, the one
with the deepest throat.

(2009)

After the Fall: Sweeping Up Snowbell Blossoms
(*Styrax Japonica*)

Long before sunrise I'm out in the yard to water
the veggies and dig up a word
for the scent of snowbells adrift on the breeze.
To deadhead the ice plant
and coral poppies.

          Like flakes they are names for
(each flower unique) the petals fall gently
at angles oblique, but never a carrot-nosed
snowbell-man. Never an angel born from the weight
of my body, supine, and the downward

                      sweep of my
arms. *By sweat of your brow shall you eat bread,*
the Creator said, and that goes, I presume,
for the lower orders. Dandelions
wrestle a path through the crack between sidewalk

and driveway. When I dig them out, armies
of microscopic ants scatter from the quake.
These snowballs enact
a stunning mistake, seedpods like acorns already
forming. Overnight,

          another midsummer avalanche;
trees standing in white up to their Japanese
ankles. Far off, a faint hint of sleighbells. Whatever
season we're in, I believe my trees are cousins
of snow peas, July linking arms with December.

(2009)

Poem Beginning with a Line from the Koran

To whomsoever God assigns no light, no light has he.
My mother dead, I did not stand and wait,
all brightness fled, nor court the infinite
but blindly walked into the stark valley
of death's shadow, fearing every evil,
refusing still to serve. You were not with
me, let me starve, deprived of saving faith.
You left me to the wiles of Your Rival.

The Enemy of Life made life unsafe,
rehearsed the true compassion I denied.
The gates of hell stand wide when I awake
in terror of the dark and frozen lake
where bodies of the unrepentant ride
under the shadow of Your rod and staff.

(2009)

That Woman

the sun stencils on sidewalks doesn't
look like me. Wherever I go, she stalks me: I'm
stuck with her shadow. She's a cripple
who leans on a shadow walker, a kind of cage, shadow
in a cave where firelight on the wall
makes universal shadows
singularly real. A second shadow

                                 armed with a scythe,
grimly closes the distance that keeps me
alive. Must I struggle always
under a bulky pack, a prisoner of shadows
who limps her way back
under tins of tuna, cucumbers, peaches
and plums? Granola?

                     Where is the confident step of
early spring? Little wonder I mourn
the lowering clouds, blackening sky: the thief
who stole her away and left
only this stranger.

(2009)

Pre-Need Planning

Caught up in details: bills for burning my bones
and delivering ashes. Cost of an urn
for the ashes and a place to keep them—I
lament this long-distance dying. Why must I choose
memorial music when the melody

                              in my ear is Today?
There's a will to be made and revised many times,
not to mention executors, literary
and other. Survivors to notify. Instructions for
letting me go

          when it's time. Barely twelve years
(my life expectancy), mind fully
engaged with the present, I'm trying to
prune my possessions, having little luck. On my
daily walk, two rows of sumac bushes on fire

arc through the schoolyard. Their red reminds me of
sanctuary lamps. Is this the shade
Moses shrank from: God in a Burning Bush?
The upward rush of light
on de la Tour Magdalens' red dresses?

                        That color
almost makes up for the iron gate, always ajar,
hazard to someone like me. I slam the gate
shut each time I pass. *Were you brought up in a
barn?* My mother would say. *Please*

close the door.
I'm trying to keep my own door open, in the shadow
of trees and vines: clematis, peonies,
snowbells, wisteria—thick stems and trunks
outpacing time. They make me

resist the third act
and the curtain call. Every seedling I plant
sprouts a wind-driven dance of survival.

(2009)

Early Work

Flotsam: Message from Mauriac

On this sandy point the seeker
May conquer the obdurate sea
And learn from her ravished innocence
The one humility.
Her sands are beset by seducers,
The same that beguile his soul
And deep in the swirling waters
Where Nature demands her toll,
The passionate currents tangle
In patterns forever prime;
While half-formed, fanciful children,
Stifled before their time,
Topple impregnable towers
Prostrate in powerless rot:
All that has been, delivered,
All that might be and is not.
Who fathoms the cloistered corruption
Under her whitened crest,
Nor blinds his eyes to her faithlessness,
Alone knows rest.
Until he can walk through the wreckage,
Untouched by fear and surprise,
Look at the face of his wayward love
And number her harlotries,
His surging strength covers quicksand,
Lining the brink of hell,
And Death makes feast in the secret depths
Where Life should dwell.

(1949)

Song for Any Magdalen

The crumpled lilies weep at Mary's feet
And frosty stars, ablur within her crown,
Toll twice unlovely death.

There will be other blooms where these have bled:
Proud purple thistles
Hedged about with pain;
And scarlet poppies stabbing through the mist
Of bitterness
That shrouds the young heart slain.

But none shall kindle blackened blooms with spring
And heal the wounded whiteness bent to earth
Until the wasted fragrance, scattered on the wind,
Awake some distant dawn to fairer birth
In lands beyond the tempests of desire;
And over dear-bought graves of innocence,
The new and regal lilies blaze white fire.

(1950)

Invitation to Renouncement

I...will lead her into the wilderness...
Hosea 2:14

Yes, welcome winter to your land
And cage the frozen bird;
Let no reluctant leaf withstand
The summons you have heard.

And open wide your doors to Night
Inexorable and soon.
Smother the stars from your greedy sight,
Bury the thin, cold moon,

And Loneliness will come to stay
Upon a Single Cross;
Dismiss the thieves, lest even they
Be counterpoise to loss.

Then seek the vaulted dark at last
And seal it with a stone
That only Heaven may venture past
To conjure up its own.

(1951)

Prayer for a Stray Shepherd

Scant thirty coins I bring,
Yet stamped with sacrifice.
Not now as Judas did,
I reckon up the price;
But here in darkness hid,
I buy the bartered Christ,
And know, since I have bid
My all, it must suffice.

(1951)

High School Students' Retreat

Over the rakish halos hangs the Silent Dove;
Beneath the smooth-brushed curls, a latent Teresa stirs.
What though our age be far removed from hers?
God is not bound. Nor Fire, nor Flood, nor Love.

An eager lad unwinds his noisy length,
A prey to inspiration and the urge to move;
He stutters cautious questions which the ears approve,
Though eyes mistrust the restless, untamed strength.

The room is warm with sun, but underneath the hush,
With reckless urgency, sweep tides and storms of grace;
The struggle marks a frowning, freckled face
Before the floodgates burst with sudden rush.

They seek the chapel long before the time,
With somewhat mixed intent, as scant statistics show:
To seek a favorite vantage point; to whisper low,
Imperious pleas or laments for youthful crime.

Ignatius would applaud this day, as soldiers must:
A ripening wealth of harvest in a world of tares;
Triumphant Michael's standard on the prison stairs,
And Lucifer's, deep-trampled in the dust.

(1952)

X Marks the Seeker

Mother undefiled, we meet
at the crossing of narrow roads you are not
except in our Girl Scout Guides:

your eyes (and ways) so even in the level light
I forget the angelic salute,
the night of the transverse stars
and the morning burst from the grave
to walk in the open street of noon.

Your words are made of water—
not those neon streams, but simply water,
clear and green and tranquil as the blue
 that joins Anouilh's Jeanne and
Baudelaire's little Old Women to
their cross-beamed source.

This makes you less my own, of course:
my crooked mirror, secret paradise
and chartered heaven. You are mine
only to flow away...like time,
like day, air, rain, sunlight,
birds, weeds, flowers
and the Seven Swords.

(1954)

Diary of Dreams

Dreams come at dawn like apple harvest,
Fruit gathered from the laden trees,
More than the heart can hold, the mind encounter,
spiced with discoveries.

Or else they fall in drifts of morning Maybloom,
Trailing a gentler fragrance in the sun,
Shy as the kiss of universal springtime's
Sweet oblivion.

In day's full light, dreams flash a jeweled challenge
To seek them out in labor and alone,
To guard against the night a thing of beauty
Cut from resisting stone.

At dusk they lie unseen in the dark cellar,
Stranger to open sky and earth's deep mine,
Aging within the shelter man has made them
Like rare old wine.

(1955)

Dispossessed

Slowly the firm sod loosened
And weathered branches tore,
Leaving the heart uprooted
Beside the sycamore.

Bare earth and blue sky barren
Grieve by the nameless tomb
Where clean roots clove the darkness
And green boughs arched the gloom.

Now tall winds hoard the secrets
That once they shed so free
And broken, broken, broken
Is the warm earth's hold on me.

(1955)

Solitaire

This is the land of inscrutable winter:
Thoughts buried deep in the drifting snow,
Silence as cold as the breath of the morning
Frosting the windows to hide what we know.

Pathways dissembled by wind-driven flurries
Mute the long footfalls that break through the dark:
Here in the trackless, inviolate wasteland,
Welcome erased by the trespasser's mark.

See how the fences stand firm round the holding,
Icicle-spiked where holes gapped wide,
Rigid as right and as brittle as beauty—
And the worn gate nailed inside!

(1955)

The Timely Writer

I wear my rubbers in July,
Fight taxes in September;
In May I Christmas shop and sigh
for June brides in December;
I keep an April Halloween,
send August valentines,
Trudge back to school in March, spring clean
When autumn glory shines.

If manuscripts have no come-back
I'll keep my seasons out of whack.

(1955)

Summer Hailstorm

Hard on the sudden cleavage of the light
The frozen daisies, stippled on the lawn,
Honor the thing they blight.

Cold and contained, impassioned spheres of white
Loose their windlash fury and are gone—
All but the desolate sting they leave upon
Petals of flowers folded for the night.

The splendor of the moment lingers long
And longer than the wound that never heals.
And who can say which love is weak, which strong:
The storm that strikes, the calm that yet reveals
The rifled flower where the tear congeals.

(1956)

The Ransom

The branches twisted back upon themselves
And clasped the trunk to make a fearful shade:
A screen so thick it stopped the flowing light
And choked the searching leaf-tips where they strayed.

Though all about, the trees grow lush and strong,
The blighted stock begets a bitter fruit
And poison, seeping earthward from the crown,
Fuses with venom hidden at the root.

Misshapen boughs sag with their lonely yield,
Foretell a dozen deaths if one tree fall;
But who would save must fence it round with love
Deeper than dark, higher than orchard wall.

(1956)

Street Lamp

The universe in a square of light,
Cut from overhanging night,
Swings on a silver filament.

And pigtailed promise skating there,
Beribboned joys in glowing air,
And love, improvident,

Wear lilting life with transient grace,
Unheedful of its sterner face,
Within their shining arc.

Taunted shadows disappear—
The night, the noises, and the fear:
One lamp reclaims the dark.

(1956)

Rehearsal

Along the shrunken bough neglect had cursed,
Fragile and indestructible, the blossom burst
To graft upon the omnipresent night
The undiminished brilliance born of thirst.

The apple tree awakens to the white
Sorcery of fragrance fused with light.
It feels the warm life rushing from the root
And knows the long forgetfulness was right.

The boldest promise buried in the shoot,
Unconscious of time's gradual pursuit,
May countermand the sunlight, but immersed
In darkness, bear its own transcendent fruit.

(1957)

Arctic Summer

The prismed pinnacles, alight in northern sun,
Proud and imperative as beauty meant to blind,
Warn of the froze weight that rides below
The iridescence of a height defined.

Hid in the secret waves, vast pediments,
Merged with the earth that moored them, wear like stone;
Tensioned within to equalize the pull
Of primal forces in their native zone.

Sunshafts glide off the surface to the sea
And crevices receive the grudging flow
To seal the web-like cracks that warmth has made
In unsuspected hollows far below.

Breakers in darkness circumscribe the base.
Slowly the melted ice solidifies
Till what it was splits wide the conquered heart
Freed of encasing compromise.

(1957)

Early Winter

Before the season of the vintage died
Enameled cold over the golden bough
Confined within an unsubstantial now
The richness of all autumns glorified.
The harvest burden bent the crusted branch
Serenely to the earth until it brushed
The snow with color, and reluctance rushed
To free its treasure in an avalanche.
The supple leaves, before their time unbound,
Circle the weightless tree abruptly bare.
Abandoned brightness crowds the hollow air
And drifts of silence bury common ground.

(1958)

Thirty-Fifth Spring

Weary of winter, too inert for spring,
A restless, hybrid Middlemarch I sing:
When jonquils pierce the frozen crust
I shake my head, knowing they must.
Yet let it not be said that earth is lost to me:
For all along the roots where life was stored,
The warm sap courses free and tardy shoots
Put out their timid green to test the sun.
In other days I met spring on the run
But now, grown wise, I wink the first alarms,
Relax and wait while sunshine wraps the farms,
While woods awake to birds' first faltering song
And streams shed ice, knowing that after long
Rehearsal for the Maid's debut,
I'll yawn a bit and stretch my arms
And rise to kiss her too.

(1958)

Metropolis

Under the neon cheer of loveless night
The dark marauders circumvent the day;
Where blinking brilliance parodies the light,
Bizarre, uneasy shadows ricochet.

Here hunger billows in the thinning blood,
Cold burrows deeper into fettered bone
And rhythms knock upon the solitude,
Insistent, echoing from steel and stone.

See where the open door spills greenish glare,
Distorting those who search the outworn sign;
And pours into the street the jangling air,
Conditioned by industrial design.

(1959)

Signals

Strung on magnetic frequencies
In aureoles of dance,
The incandescent snowflakes
Suffuse our small pretense.

Bewilderingly simple
And born to last a breath,
They range the tall uncertainties
To how sublime a death.

(1959)

Torque

Those intervals when motion
may substitute for light,
rain leaps from every puddle,
not beautiful nor bright,
but linked by premonition
in endless rounding riddle
with secrets of the night.

The curving of a second
traces a lingering mark
or disappears in nearness
to do a wider work
along the rim, unreckoned
by those whose final clearness
depends upon the dark.

(1960)

Small Change from the Routine Classroom

We watch your coined word flip
into the casual air,
study the light rebounding from its planes—
polygonal and polished
with a flair for bold ambivalence
that gains with height.

Falling, the disc divides,
breaks into bright
disparities that mirror what it hides;
seizes the fractured image of one face
in that enduring motion wherewith wings
lose and retrieve the solid common place
to sound the ready ear with echoings.

Or pitches to a silence,
improbable when caught:
by hands too swift for seeing
turned penny for our thought.

(1960)

Dead Letter

Enveloped in waves of sound
tuned to the absent ear,
bold as the durable bond
thought seeks the stratosphere.

My dreams and dooms and fears
wrapped in the cryptic word
wander the alien airs
intangible, unheard.

How shall the fair address
startle the eye awake
where only the empty house
answers the timid knock?

Shifted from city to town,
pleading its simple claim
the letter remains unknown,
sealed with a foreign name.

Returning, it bears the strange
mark of my signature:
fixity free to range
earth under the polar star.

(1961)

All Great Poets Are Inspired

Shooting off at the typewriter doesn't make poems:
a lesson elementary as any name. And yet
the keys contrive a pseudo-live response
to restless fingers lost in reflex dark.
Four, five, six lines to a stanza.
The fingers chop them off
at ragged intervals,
more play than work, calculated to the syllable,
off-rhymes tucked in, casual as a split-level
ranch house with no stairs to climb.

For two cents I'd throw the whole thing over.
For a dime I'd manufacture sonnets. But for free,
I'll bungle along
impaled on that incredible romance
like a broken record
tossing its snatch of dissonance.
Or a stray chord shifted out of key,
identity unestablished, no name and no address:
I know a poem neither more nor less
than I know a typewriter's fixed, irregular lines,
a stolen chance,
and the hovering trigger finger shooting off.

(1961)

Winter Song

Out of stillness deep as sunken stone
light comprehends the night's intended drift:
clear stars that find their certitude alone
strike glory from the planets till the afterimage
widens to the stirred pool's rim.
O lightly rides the heavens' weight
(as Spirit broods and starbirds skim)
where waters sing under their burden of delight
the Virgin Mother's flowering.

(1962)

After Harvest

The slow fires rouse though all the fields are down
Where stubble tells the reaping black and plain;
Impassioned harvests stir in blowing ash
The golden ghosts of grain.

Fingers of fire no longer than a wish
Sigh to a close around the unbound shock
Touching to consciousness the single spear
Where the rain-ripe year awoke

To voices of the wind in a stranded ear,
Bright kernels rounding surely for the sheaf
Against the sunframed day they meet their match
And green flames tremble on the stalk of grief.

(1962)

Between Seasons

Now with the coming of the wind
I know where darkness moves: moves everywhere.
No winter's warmth shored up with song and dream
waits to redeem
gusts of indifferent air.

Gold light of maples wet beneath our feet
predicts a pattern for the full-fleshed grape:
rocking in trellised mirth, leaves sway and sprawl
above a falling
petal-stained and vacant earth.

Too quick for death, too stark for sleep
this stillness breeds calamity, not storm,
where life leaks out unsummoned from the vine
whose tendrils twine
rigor of senseless form.

(1962)

Cashmere

Train wheels from decades past click into
the station where snow wraps a thick
scarf around the neck of the streetlamp.
I am on my way to obscure platforms, worlds
too remote to remember. If I have
arrived, send word, send a search party.
Tell them to look near the tracks
where the snow goes on falling.

(1962)

Campus Planning

Repetitive along the mall, four trees
at ease, predictable, turn traffic back
as stoplights once returned a wilderness.
First, the larch, hybrid and plumy, surmounting
its railroad ties and rechristened tamarack.
The obsequies rain down as needles drop.

Then, the magnolia. Each with its five-foot circle
of earth attached to a mine of coarse roots and fine
that the spring will explode, and wrapped up in sacks
from a load of potatoes stamped with the state
and a blue-lettered Smoothie.

Deodar next. A wooden god, propped up
to keep things tidy and, seen from west-
northeast, convincing. The tides are scarcely
that: all seasons surge, too dense
to classify in this coastal climate. Fogbound
and seldom dry, the woods keep hardly green.

Our homegrown nurseryman's a man of God.
He names the trees and knows the seasons in their turn
and plots the squares where plants will be supplied
with food and trimmed at proper intervals to keep
from getting out of hand.

The fourth tree, birch or beech or Irish yew:
a specialty preserved according to its kind.
Lop off the lower limbs and nothing's dead.
Isolate in brick-walled nooks, instead
of scrub, shrublets. In disciplined cement
a prospect dearly bought.

Nearby, the squat
yellow man, freely translated, peering out
from the epicanthus, borrows the rain's pitch
for an old commission: *Thou art the gardener*
and deep in devouring asphalt
I will sink my trees.

(1962)

Christianizing the Chapel

Determined to rebuild by Christmas Eve
we sent for the architect, the Carpenters'
Union, the Electrician's Guild, and told
them: Save this battle-scarred monument;
reconcile the contradictions and make
the product of historic wars into
a house of peace we can believe in.

Ecumenical by design (synthetic
synagogue with plaster Catholic saints)
a welter of conflicting line
half fiberboard, half knotty pine—an Air
Force Classic—everything but Greek. But if
you thought your suffering unique, an honest-to-god
hand-carved crucifix to show up the fraud.

On Monday they crashed through the wall and found remnants
of contending forces—soldiers all and true—
Alleluias bumping into penitential
psalms; Yom Kippur lighting candles for
the Mass, and a stalwart champion of Reform
bouncing anathemas off a pillar
in uneasily familiar style.

The carpenters stripped supports of bric-a-brac
getting down to basics, followed the clean line
of the room and the beamed ceiling, sealed off scattered
exits, yanked out a railing, ripped up partitions,
took a crowbar to ceremonial platforms that propped
us up, revealing the planked floor under our
stumbling feet, substantial as an ox.

Less than brilliant, the wooly light of a winter
afternoon opens out on amazing mysteries
lost in the ordinary dazzle of fluorescence.
Hammerblows and the nerve-fraying whine
of the drill disappear. A wave of cold air washes in
to settle the sawdust and the chapel falls still.
Empty and waiting, it yawns like a hillside cave.

(1962)

The Poem

Straight on, the cat.

Plucked from a jungle
of road repair
his amber eyes
hung for a second's warning
in the glare of headlights
trained through mist.
The city swerved away
from that forest. I read the signs
and knew too much too late:
the cat's-eye lanterns
giving off false clues
and sawhorse guardians
barring deeper dark.

Only the animal was real.
The wheel borrowed his rhythms
in my hand—
a kind of power steering
pointed towards fate.
On the Idaho border
I can appreciate
those last-chance markers,
reverse direction
and go meet the inevitable
even in a hearse.

Nightmare, reality or vision:
whatever he was, I found him.
I'd made my decision,
or had it made for me,
in the blinding moment
before the crash.

(1962)

A Fabulous Poem

A slice of intransigent moon
cut through the general fog
proclaiming, "The sawed-off world's
still shining and sure at the top."

A million stars had
remembered to stop
where the confident mist uncurled
around and along the invincible bough
and the fountains of tropical green.
(For everyone knew that the truest real
is the real that
cannot be seen.)

All the plumed heads bobbed
in the global night
and floated on fog at dawn.
And the people said,
"This remarkable state of affairs
cannot go on."

While the worm at work in the severed soil
angled his way to a bird
the loosened roots
in the dark below
let go
and the fog was stirred.

(1963)

Montana Legend

Fenced in by fierce names and federal law
Montana hoards its dole of wilderness
scaled to the pitch of a disappearing cry
that borrows mountain passes for a megaphone
or bounces urgent signals from the towered rock.

Sure-footed by necessity, I prowl
that privileged waste, unable to shake my shadow
even on moonless nights. Nothing will answer back
that's not my own. Stalked by a possible dawn
I sign a mountain spine with my epitaph.

Into that landscape introduce two modes of locomotion designed
for trackless travel and the gratuitous landing—to wit, the absurd
and clumsily inventive whirly bird, complemented (oddly)
by the mechanistic mule.

Now a helicopter's a hybrid
as every schoolboy knows—
predictably difficult on difficult days—
reversible, long-eared, voice that brays.
Stationary at need, and need unspecified,
saddled with miscellaneous ware
and given the time, driven anywhere.

The mule, on the other hand, was invented for all
those important but eccentric missions that would
make a blimp curvet and a jet limp.

An engineer can blast a rocket
to the moon and reappear
by teatime, but it takes
a mountainous poet to lift a mule
over those Montana forests
without being thrown.

It was easier once when Pegasus kicked up springs
and those who hankered after the heavens' riddle
like Bellerophon, slept at Athena's shrine and woke
to a golden bridle that would charm the marvellous beast.
Like a native son made lord of the air, he won confidence
to kill chimaeras—though, to be mythematically exact, he
tried to fly too high and ended up—intact, but barely—de-
vouring his own soul, avoiding the paths of men.

Montana gives me room to try again.

(1964)

Afterword

Afterward

In emails back and forth about this Afterword, I've found myself mistyping it as "Afterward." Maybe that's fitting. It comes at the end of this book, which comes at the end of all the other projects I've done for Madeline as her literary executor. This is the last, and then my work will be finished. It will all be Afterward, after this.

I knew Madeline nearly all my life. She was my parents' friend before she was mine. She and my dad both started teaching at the University of Montana in the fall of 1967. Her long friendship with my parents began inauspiciously. When I asked, none of them remembered their first meeting. I'm told I was there, but I was (at most) eighteen months old.

Some of my earliest memories are of Madeline. Before she was my model of what a poet could be, she was my model of what a grownup could be—open, curious, delighted by everything. She always bent down to talk to me on my level. She always had little gifts in her pocket she'd set aside for my brother and me— stickers, buttons, the tiny porcelain animals that came in boxes of Red Rose tea. She was always smiling.

I know from reading her journals that those first years in Missoula were dazzling and fraught—she was euphoric over her new-found freedoms one minute and anxious, guilt-ridden, despairing the next. I think that's why she came so often to our house to talk to my mother, a counselor by training, and why she so often showed her drafts to my father, who was an excellent reader and more importantly, not a poet, not a member of the English department, not in competition with her in any way. But I'm getting ahead of myself.

Madeline was a nun when she got to Missoula, and she wasn't a nun when she left. That was Richard Hugo's line. He was teaching at Montana already, and recommended Madeline to replace him for a year while he went to Italy on a Rockefeller grant. She said he wasn't threatened by her, so she made the perfect candidate, one who wouldn't steal his job. She didn't but was asked to remain on the faculty and stayed until 1979, when she moved east to direct the creative writing program at the

University of Massachusetts, Amherst. In the interim, she requested a dispensation from her vows in 1973. She was fifty-four. I remember having to learn to call her "Madeline" instead of "Sister Madeline." That's all I remember. I was seven.

There was so much I didn't know about her life. Even after years of listening to her stories and after interviewing her a couple of times, I've spent much of the last decade piecing together her history while reading and rereading her published work, organizing her papers and editing a collection of her essays, some of which explore this period in depth.

When Madeline arrived in Missoula in 1967, she was forty-seven, she had an M.A. in journalism, and she'd published three books under the name Sister Mary Gilbert: two convent memoirs and her first poetry collection, *From the Darkroom* (Bobbs-Merrill, 1964). She'd taught for several years at Holy Names College in Spokane. But she'd never lived alone, never learned how to cook or drive or manage her own money, and she knew nothing about popular culture. (She'd entered the Congregation of the Sisters of the Holy Names of Jesus and Mary in 1936, so she'd missed *a lot* of popular culture.)

By the time my parents met her, Madeline no longer wore the habit. Thanks to the modernizing influence of the Vatican II council, she'd gotten permission to wear regular clothes and reclaim her baptismal name just before she got to Montana (though she said every time she returned to Spokane she had to "leap back into the habit," to avoid giving the other sisters ideas). She had permission to live away from the community in a furnished apartment her superior chose for her, but all her income continued to go to the community. When she learned to drive, the community bought a car for her use. She wasn't allowed to own anything (or to consider anything she had truly hers—that was sometimes an easier way to think about it).

The rules and practices of the community were often difficult to interpret or follow in her new context, and she didn't want to jeopardize her independence by asking too many questions. It was all very isolating. In her essay, "The Cryptic Language of the Private Poet," she described "the acute sense of exile...when [she] received the community newsletter and found no mention of those...living and working apart from the group at a time when such forays were infrequent." After living in community for thirty-two years, she was thrilled to be on her own. She also felt cut off, ignored, forgotten—and often lonely.

The Congregation of the Sisters of the Holy Names of Jesus and Mary is a teaching order. These were the nuns who taught Madeline in high school, at St. Mary's Academy in Portland, Oregon. St. Mary's was a formative place for her. She talked her parents into letting her board with her uncle's family in Portland so she could attend—it was too far to commute from Hillsboro, which was then a farming town of three thousand people. The nuns at St. Mary's were better educated than any of her grade school teachers, there was an excellent library and a librarian who fed her challenging books, and her classmates admired both her wit and her poems. She always attributed her command of the sentence and the line to her senior English teacher, whose rigorous adherence to the imitative exercises in *Model English* gave her a solid foundation.

I don't fully understand all Madeline's reasons for becoming a nun. She had deep faith, certainly. She mentioned to me once that she didn't want to follow her mother's traditional path—marriage, children, a house to keep—but there weren't many other paths available in 1936, or if there were, she didn't know about them. Still, the emotional, intuitive piece of her decision always eluded me, until I read her description of a moment in the St. Mary's chapel "in which [she] felt most fully alive:"

> ...here in the heart of light, the traffic seemed as remote as
> the hum of a plane on the other side of the
> sound barrier.
>
> I was learning the inner stillness that links poetry and prayer.
> ("The Cryptic Language of the Private Poet")

Her relief in this atmosphere is palpable. Stillness was in short supply at home in Hillsboro, where her anxious, overbearing mother filled every silence with chatter. As a child, Madeline often hid under the dining room table or in the attic, desperate for a little privacy. In interviews, she said her mother "would have liked to know my every thought!" and when she began writing poems, they became a "private place" where she could keep those thoughts to herself.

Perhaps Madeline's two vocations, poetry and religious life, became entangled and confused because she traced them back to the same, early source—her time at St. Mary's. Or perhaps there was no confusion. She was very young, always a year younger than the others in her class because she'd started first grade at five instead of six. Her sense of what her sacrifice meant was idealistic, even romantic (which the rhetoric and ritual—becoming a "bride of Christ," wearing a plain gold band— did nothing to dispel).

"I went into the convent just out of high school at sixteen, persuaded that in doing so, I sacrificed a promising literary career to some nobler calling," she wrote in "Letter to a Young Woman Artist." Later she came to believe, as Merton did, that "poetry was not so much something one did as it was a part of who a person was." The sacrifice of her *self* was a far greater sacrifice, with graver consequences, than the career she thought she'd forfeited.

From the beginning, convent life afforded Madeline little time for writing. Her days were long and heavily scheduled between common prayer, teaching, chores, and communal recreation. Initially, she taught elementary school during the year (a high school diploma was the only credential required in those days) and took classes during the summers at Marylhurst College. It took her eleven years to complete her BA. Meanwhile, she stole time for writing when she could.

> On my knees, I polished the lines clean as I dusted a flight of stairs and tried to chase them from my head while I meditated in a drafty chapel shortly after five each morning. To clear my head for the next stanza, I scribbled the first on a used envelope after dormitory lights blinked out at 9:25 p.m. I walked from convent to classroom comatose, looking for a better word, a truer image. I pecked at an antique typewriter during infrequent hours when the others watched a movie certified suitable for nuns in the common recreation room. At intervals I timidly broached the subject of my buried talent and tried to accept the need to make pedagogy a priority. Between these times I reflected on Hopkins' elected silence and wondered when conscience or counsel would force me to fall mute.
> ("Letter to a Young Woman Artist")

Even after she had enough seniority to request magazine subscriptions, money for postage and occasional classes in support of her writing—she had to be careful that what she wrote would be considered appropriate. Her work couldn't be personal or prideful, and some feelings were not acceptable—a nun was expected to be "sunny and reposeful," and to blend in with the community, not stand out.

> ...the exercise of literary and artistic talent was often considered self-willed, an interference with common life and the real work of the order. Such activity was to be blessed by obedience, channeled often into utilitarian projects such as the manufacture of coffee mugs and pious statues, of greeting cards, inspirational pamphlets, and edifying biographies of dead monks and nuns. Serious art too easily became a threat and a distraction. ("Monks Pond and the Slough of Despair")

So why did she remain in the community for thirty-eight years, long after she began to have doubts about her true vocation? *The Springs of Silence,* the memoir of convent life Madeline published in 1953, helped me understand what made it so difficult for her to decide to leave. In two remarkable chapters, she describes undergoing a profound spiritual crisis and wrestling, ostensibly for the first time, with her fears about trying to begin again as an ex-nun.

Madeline's good friend Pat Solon, also a former sister of the Holy Names of Jesus and Mary, reminded me that she wrote this book on assignment as a recruiting tool for the Congregation. Also, spiritual crises were more common in the community than this book made them out to be. Anytime one of the sisters left, the rest were likely to suffer doubts about their own commitment. The crisis Madeline describes as taking place in 1948, twelve years after she entered the community, was probably not her first.

Still, Madeline's disillusionment and sense of failure ring true, as do her worries about letting down her friends in the convent and disappointing her parents, who were proud to have a nun in the family. She wonders whether she could ever "readjust to the world."

So many things about it would seem strange and foolish.

Wherever I went, people would look at each other and whisper, "She used to be a nun." They might be polite, but they could scarcely help being curious.

How would I ever be able to endure their questions? Would I ever learn to be anything but a self-conscious misfit?

She was right about the curiosity—those questions never ceased. But what ultimately held her back was the finality of the decision.

The obvious thing to do was to apply for dispensation, but that was the one thing I could not compel myself to do.

It was such an irrevocable step—more so, in one way, than the making of the final vows had been.

For I knew that, once outside, there would be no question of my return.

The doors swing out more easily than they swing in.

In the narrative, Madeline marks the resolution of this spiritual crisis by writing "Flotsam: Message from Mauriac," which appeared in the Catholic magazine, *Spirit*, in 1949 (and is included here in the Early Work section). She reprinted the poem in *The Springs of Silence*, where its riot of erotic imagery is at odds with her assertion that its subject is the grace of forgiveness and love. At ninety, she was dismayed when I asked if she considered this her first mature poem ("I don't like to think of it as exemplary in any way!"), but she could still recite it in its entirety. I believe it was the first poem she published in which she expressed her frustration and grief, though of course she didn't want it to be read that way at the time.

Madeline's early work (1949-1964) fascinates me. Her superiors looked favorably on writing that brought in any extra income, so initially she focused on short humor pieces and light verse she could sell to general-interest magazines like *The Saturday Evening Post*. Many of the shorter poems in the Early Work section of this book she sold to *The New York Times*—in the era of moveable type, they kept a supply of "fillers" to insert in a column with room to spare. She published poems on religious themes in Catholic magazines like *Spirit*. However safe the subject (nature, weather, and seasons were the top three, apart from religion), all of these poems are marked by an intensity of diction, a sense of pressure behind the words and emotionally charged images that would otherwise tend toward cliché.

In 1959, Madeline took a poetry workshop with Karl Shapiro that was a turning point for her. She'd had the ambition to write more seriously for some time. He encouraged her to try free verse, and to work towards her first collection:

> Karl Shapiro...told me to publish a book of poems...and promised to take some poems for *Prairie Schooner*. That summer Nelson Bentley of the University of Washington gave me a big boost on the road to publication, and a year or two later, Father Michael McAniff helped me along with reading and repeated assurances that the emergence of woman was the greatest single phenomenon in three hundred years... Mother Mary Joan, a sympathetic provincial superior, who might have been a writer herself had she been given the opportunity, urged me to keep on writing, and [Sister] Bernadette Carlson, a poet in her own right, reinforced my determination in her triple role as friend, superior, and college president. ("Letter to a Young Woman Artist")

Madeline craved a larger community of writers, even as she shrank from their scrutiny. In the summer of 1961, she went to study with John Berryman and Robert Fitzgerald at the Indiana University School of Letters. She was self-conscious about not being as well read as the other students, and conspicuous as a nun in habit. Berryman bullied her, as he was known to do, and she struggled, but she found an important ally in one of her fellow students, Bruce Jackson.

She was still "writing in code," as she put it, to preserve her privacy and to evade censorship, but Bruce was a more sensitive reader than most:

> One day he looked up from the page to ask, "What do the other sisters think when they see these poems?"
>
> "They think they're not reading what they're reading." And I felt a rush of relief, in spite of all my efforts at concealment, to know that I was now being read truly.
>
> The usual response of my companions was bafflement—that of outsiders, stereotypical. With too many outsiders, I could write about murder and it would be read as martyrdom. ("Resolution and Independence: John Berryman's Ghost and the Meaning of Life")

By the time Madeline's first poetry collection, *From the Darkroom*, came out in 1964, she'd published a second memoir, *Later Thoughts from the Springs of Silence*, on moving Holy Names College to Fort Wright in Spokane. She'd also had some success with her fiction, and one of her stories had been included in *Best American Short Stories* of 1962.She longed to be taken seriously as a poet and had high hopes for the book, but according to her, it "sank without a trace."

In a 1980 essay, "Domesticating Two Landscapes: The Poetry of Madeline DeFrees," M.L. Lewandowska and Susan Baker admired the craft of these early poems, but felt they reflected the restrictions of the cloister, observing that Madeline "...kept her self within a splendid cage of form," and "[s]he said much, but she stoppered up more...." Like all her early work, the poems in *From the Darkroom* depict "a world of hush, of numbness, of objectification:"

> There are, for example, no individuals; there are people, yes, but only
> nuns in groups, strangers on a bus, two "he's" ...and one "Irish
> poet"...time is measured not by events, but by the passage of seasons.
> Sometimes seasonal changes in landscape are abstracted to provide
> metaphors for a sense of being trapped in time...Other seasonal changes
> are made concrete...Yet the limitation remains; this is still a generalized
> landscape.

The opening poems in *Where the Horse Takes Wing* are from an unfinished sequence, "A Catch of Summer," that Madeline began in the summer of 1964. She was living on campus at Holy Names College and had been given time and space to work on her writing. The sections never came together as a single piece, but they served to test new styles and focus, as well as a new approach. In an unfinished essay on the poetic sequence, she described her process:

> Mornings, I worked on [fiction] at the typewriter in the journalism office.
> Afternoons, I took a yellow legal pad and pen to a small explosives cabin
> on the Fort property, situated in the wilder part. I opened the padlock on
> the cabin door, lit a candle because there was no electricity in the small
> space, and sat in the doorway after my "walk in the woods" working on
> poems.

The landscape of these poems is unmistakably the Holy Names campus at Fort Wright in Spokane, bounded on one side by railroad tracks and still harboring remnants of its military past. The poet who "takes a stand" in the Section I is initially male, perhaps a nod to Hayden Carruth, whose long sequence Madeline read in the *Virginia Quarterly Review* that summer, and whose method inspired her own—walking, then working from images collected along the way. The action, however, is all interior. The tone shifts dramatically between the first and third sections, as Madeline comes to terms with her desire to leave religious life and commit fully to being a poet. She won't act on it for nearly a decade, but this is her rehearsal—a summer spent vanquishing straw men ("a troop of tumbleweed taller than any fear") until "no longer afraid of our shadows...." She ends with the victor in that contest, "the poet / who pondered the summer and won."

I also began *Where the Horse Takes Wing* with "A Catch of Summer" because it embodies the choice she's making to "fall" away from God and plunge—fearfully, joyfully—into a different life.

Madeline mentions "the first fall," in Section III of "A Catch of Summer:" the scent of mock-orange "...hangs / on the air like a forgotten / number or the first fall." A later section, "In the Scales: I" makes a more pointedly biblical reference that ends with the line: "I turn my face to the fall," which echoes Isaiah 38:2, in which Hezekiah "turns his face to the wall." In this passage, Hezekiah is ill and Isaiah tells him: "Set your house in order for you shall die and not live." He turns his face to the wall and weeps and prays to the Lord, "I have walked before You in truth and with a loyal heart, and have done what is good in Your sight." The Lord grants him fifteen more years of life, and in gratitude—Hezekiah writes a poem.

I didn't include section IV because she published it as a stand-alone poem, retitled: "Everything Starts with the Fall," in her second book, *Where Sky Lets Go* (George Braziller, 1978).

Madeline's insistence on claiming her fall, her failure, has led some readers to believe she chose poetry over her religious beliefs, but she never left the Catholic Church. She was a faithful parishioner all her life, and her faith informed—but didn't dictate—everything she wrote. She explained herself by saying both religious life and poetry were "absolute vocations" and that she'd had to choose because you can have only one. But there was more to "the fall" than that. She'd made a life-long commitment to God, and even a Papal dispensation couldn't nullify that. She remained accountable to God for her broken vows, and she continued to claim her decision as both a failure and a new beginning in poems that also celebrate her "deep roots in the clay of / the human." ("Inmates Arrested in the Garden")

Once on her own, living and teaching in Missoula, Madeline became increasingly accountable to herself for her own "lost selves," and sought to recover them "from the self imposed by thirty-eight years in the convent." The poems from this period, 1967 to 1979, are some of my favorites, as intense as the exhilarating new experiences that fueled them. Poems like "The Least Romantic" and "Sunday Service" are filled with vivid sketches of people she knew and place names that clearly situate the poems in and around Missoula. In them, Madeline claims the feelings and sense of herself she'd subordinated all through her convent years and asserts their validity in language that is bold and concrete. In poems like "The Way Back," she writes as one who still feels vulnerable and voiceless ("Fog, cool at my throat, / muffles my voice...") but is beginning to muster some bravado:

> In a roadbed overgrown
> with spiked grass and wild roses, some trespassing
> was called for.

It was clear that, on balance, she relished her new life. As she wrote in "A Regular Deposit to Your Savings Account," "Risk is its own reward."

When trying to explain what made her transition to independence so difficult, Madeline often invoked Erving Goffman's 1961 book, *Asylums: Essays on the Social Situation of Mental Patients and Other Inmates.* Goffman's definition of a "total institution" was one that subjugated free will almost entirely by dictating schedules, tasks, clothing and food. Such choices then became overwhelming once an individual was living "outside" again.

This describes life in the convent before Vatican II, when "the pressures towards uniformity in insignificant matters" were most intense. "For instance, the Rule and Book of Customs regulated even minute details of external deportment: the length of one's stride, the expression of the countenance, the position of the hands." ("Monks Pond and the Slough of Despair: Crisis in the Cloister and the Flight from the Feminine") By the time significant reforms were being made in the mid- to late-1960s, Madeline was on her way out.

She also recognized that her circumstance as a single woman both liberated and constrained her:

> ...my emergence from the cloister gives me a strong bond with women whose lives were superficially very different from mine. I know how that housebound mother, newly divorced, feels when she suddenly has to come to grips with independent living. I know the problems of learning—or relearning—how to drive at fifty, the difficulties of budget and finance, of credit and real estate, machines and repairs, dealing with a society built for couples. (Interview, Rosemary Sullivan, 1980)

Even after Madeline was well-established in her academic career, she had to jockey for position on faculties that were mostly male. She was paid less and sometimes asked to shoulder extra departmental responsibilities because she didn't have the responsibility of a family. Her financial situation was already precarious—she had entered the workforce in middle age, with no savings of her own, and no right to the money she earned before she received a dispensation from her vows in 1973. The move to Massachusetts in 1979 nearly wiped out six years of savings, and she had to begin again, scrimping to put money away for her retirement, which was fast approaching.

Confidence, under these conditions, continued to be a complex process of advance and retreat, finding the courage to write and then losing it, again and again. The self-doubt Madeline chronicled in her journals stands in marked contrast to the visible successes she'd had by this time. Her third full-length collection, *Magpie on the Gallows*, came out in 1982 from Copper Canyon Press. She'd been awarded grants by both the National Endowment for the Arts and the Guggenheim Foundation, and spent the bulk of that academic year 1982-83 on the Oregon coast, working on a sequence of poems that would appear in *Shenandoah* and *The Paris Review* before being published in its entirety as *The Light Station on Tillamook Rock* (Arrowwood Press, 1989).

When Madeline returned to Massachusetts in 1983 after her Guggenheim year, she found new inspiration in the nineteenth century diaries of New England "whaling wives," who accompanied their husbands on whaling expeditions. Neither genteel society nor their husbands' shipboard crews valued the intelligence and courage of these women, and they struggled to find their place on land and at sea. Adapting to the expectations and restrictions of one world invariably made them unfit for the other—a plight familiar to Madeline.

She began a series of persona poems, drawing on the diaries for the voices and circumstances of her invented characters. They offered a means to explore all the roles her own choices had precluded. Desire Hathaway and Submit Claiborne are both wives and mothers, and Madeline chronicles their hardships and loneliness through the "unattended terrors" of giving birth and the loss of a child.

Jenny Martinson is childless and uneducated. ("She is based on Annie Ricketson, a semi-literate character," Madeline wrote in a letter to Carolyn Kizer. A bound photocopy of Annie Ricketson's diary was among Madeline's books.) Jenny is also the least encumbered by class expectations—or the least observant of them. She seems free to study shipboard life and the sights in port, and her descriptions are by far the most colorful. Her lively interest in every new discovery reminds me of Madeline in Missoula, and I suspect Annie/Jenny also appealed to Madeline because of her own blue-collar beginnings.

Three of these poems were published, but Madeline put the others aside until I found them in her files in 2009. She said she'd told a colleague at U Mass she was working on them, and his only response was, "Why?" She'd also sent drafts to some of her friends in the winter and spring of 1984. Carolyn Kizer's comments were encouraging, though she criticized some of the language ("a little dead here and there..."). Tess Gallagher was more enthusiastic ("you have again, as with *Imaginary Ancestors*, found a very original way of coming to material nobody else has come to"). Unfortunately, Helen Vendler had just published an essay in *Poetry*, disparaging the persona poem as "literary ventriloquism," which made Madeline question her project. I'm not sure, on balance, what kept her from finishing the sequence. When I asked her about it in 2009, she only quoted me that single, male voice, asking, "Why?"

When Madeline retired from the University of Massachusetts, Amherst, in 1985 and moved to Seattle, she made a conscious choice to dedicate her remaining years to writing. She still taught an occasional class, was featured at residencies, and briefly joined the faculty of the Pacific low-residency MFA program. But mostly, she wrote.

That was when I got to know her again, as an adult. I moved to Seattle in 1989. I'd visited her with my parents shortly after she settled into the house in Ballard, and it seemed only natural to call her up and get back in touch. She was never too busy for lunch, and recommended books, invited me to readings, introduced me to her friends. I wasn't writing yet myself and I didn't know much about poetry, but it was obvious even to me that at seventy, she was a writer at the height of her powers. And then at eighty, and beyond.

She published four full-length collections in retirement: *Imaginary Ancestors* (Broken Moon Press, 1990), *Possible Sibyls* (Lynx House Press, 1991), *Blue Dusk: New and Selected Poems 1951-2001* (Copper Canyon Press, 2001), which was awarded the Lenore Marshall Award from the Academy of American Poets and the Washington State Book Award for Poetry, and *Spectral Waves* (Copper Canyon Press, 2006) which earned her a second Washington State Book Award for Poetry when she was eighty-seven years old.

Madeline asked me to be her literary executor in 2007, and over the next couple of years, I went to her house every Friday to sort and file and ask questions—though first, we'd share a sandwich or a cup of tea and talk. I got to know her then better than I ever had. When she moved out of her house in 2009, most of her papers and publications (around fifty boxes) came to live with me. When she moved to Portland in 2010, I took her poetry library as well, twenty-two boxes of books that eventually went to the Maureen and Mike Mansfield Library at the University of Montana, where they're shelved with the Poetry Corner collection. The rest of her books—fiction, nonfiction, and reference—went to Folio, a private athenium in Seattle.

Madeline left the bulk of her archive to the University of Massachusetts, Amherst, Libraries, and I shipped it to them in September 2018, almost eleven years to the day I first went down to her basement office, opened a file drawer, and began my work. She threw nothing away and had never used a computer, so her archive was remarkably complete and almost entirely paper. In the end, it comprised thirty-six boxes—950 lbs. of paper—and twenty-five additional pieces, including broadsides and posters, original art from her books, her Blue Nun bar mirrors and the scrapbook her mother kept of her first clippings.

I imagine that if Madeline been able to keep writing into her nineties, she might have built her ninth collection around her late poems about aging, poems about the daily indignities of forgetfulness and lost objects, physical diminishment, falls and injury—poems like "Physical Therapy," "That Woman," and "Pre-Need Planning." Many are small masterpieces, closely observed, uncompromising and sometimes bleak, though not without grace notes, a touch of humor or simply an image like "Putting a flat hat on one's sorrow." ("Climbing the skybridge stair on my way to Suzzallo Library")

She'd probably have included some of the earlier poems that were never collected, poems like "Romantic Period" or "Safari," that dealt with late love and its disappointments. Maybe they seemed too personal at the time, or just didn't fit the manuscript then underway. Perhaps she'd have resurrected the Whaling Wives and tried to finish the sequence. She did sometimes revise her opinion of older poems, or the poems themselves. She might have felt the Whaling Wives' time had come. I'd say their time has never passed.

As I've put this book together, I've often thought back to the ambitious young poet who wrote "A Catch of Summer." It's her I always picture, "framed in illusions of the open door," steeling herself to go alone into the unknown. She found the courage to walk through that door to the rest of her life, not once but repeatedly. She tore down the walls she carried within her, and that too, she had to do repeatedly. It took enormous will, every time, to write what angered and shamed her, what was frail and flawed and human. But that's what mattered to her.

In "Pre-Need Planning," one of the last poems she published, she wrote, "I'm trying to keep my own door open,"

> resist the third act
> and the curtain call. Every seedling I plant
> sprouts a wind-driven dance of survival.

Poetry was the means *and* the end for Madeline. She survived by writing these poems. She survived to write these poems. Now only the poems survive. It's been my privilege to gather them into this book, which I offer now to you.

Anne McDuffie
December 1, 2018

Acknowledgements

We gratefully acknowledge the following publications and anthologies in which some of these poems previously appeared:

Agni Review, Aspen Leaves, Basalt, Calapooya Collage, Calapooya, Carbuncle, Catholic School Journal, Catholic World, College Composition and Communication, Columbia, Commonweal, Crab Creek Review, Cutbank, Driftwood, Exhibition, Fire on Her Tongue: An Anthology of Contemporary Women's Poetry (Two Sylvias Press, 2011), *Fragments, Garret, GiltEdge, Good Housekeeping, Graham House Review, Hubbub, Human Voice, Hurakan, Image: Prose and Poetry by Northwest Writers* (Seattle Arts Commission, 1992), *Indiana Review, Jeopardy, Literary Review, Massachusetts Review, Minnesota Review, Modern Poetry of Western America: An Anthology* (Brigham Young University Press, 1975), *Montana Women Writers: A Geography of the Heart* (Farcountry Press, 2006), *New American Review, The New York Times, Nimrod, North Dakota Quarterly, Northwest Review, Norwottock, Ohio University Review, Oregon East, Perspective: A Quarterly of Literature and the Arts, Ploughshares, The Poet's Choice, 100 American Poets' Favorite Poems* (Green Harbor: Tendril, 1980), *Poetry Northwest, Puerto del Sol, Reflection, Rendezvous, Saturday Review, Scarecrow Poetry: The Muse in Post-Middle Age* (The Ashland Poetry Press, 1994), *Scratchgravel Hills, Sewanee Review, Shenandoah, Sign, Signals, The Southern Review, Spirit, Spirituality & Health, St. Andrew's Review, Stafford's Road* (Adrienne Lee Press, 1991), *Suisun Valley Review, Tar River Poetry, The Joyce Kilmer Anthology of Catholic Poetry* (Doubleday: Image Books, 1959), *The Pacific, The Sandhills/St. Andrew's Review, The Sound of a Few Leaves: An Appointment Book of Weeks and Anthology of Current Poetry* (The Rook Press, 1977), *The Stream Invents a Smile* (Montana Arts Council Poets and Writers in Schools Program, 1980), *Today, University of Portland Review, Volt, Woman Poet—the West,"* Vol. *I* (Regional Editions: Women-in-Literature, 1980), *The Wrighter, Writer's Digest,* and *Yes Poetry.*

My thanks to Kelli Russell Agodon and Annette Spaulding-Convy for suggesting this book and making it happen. Thanks also to Kathleen, Dennis and James Wang for permission to use the woodcut their father, the artist Hui-Ming Wang, created from Madeline's poem in 1979.

I'm grateful to the librarians and archivists at the Maureen and Mike Mansfield Library at the University of Montana, The Montana Historical Society, Seton Hall University Archives, Lockwood Library at the University of Buffalo, and to Rick Newby, who all helped me track down poems and dates.

I'm indebted to all Madeline's friends, former students, colleagues and editors who've helped along the way and continue to champion her work: Sandra Alcosser, Karen Maeda Allman, Elizabeth Austen, Dorothy Barresi, Candace Black, Laurie Blauner, Sharon Bryan, Christine Deaval, Alice Derry, Laura Jensen, Chris Higashi, Christopher Howell, William Kittredge, Jennifer Maier, John W. Marshall, Frances McCue, Rick Robbins, Lex Runciman, Rick Simonson, Kim Stafford, Tree Swenson, Gary and Linda Thompson, Elizabeth Weber, Lois Welch, Michael Wiegers, Carolyne Wright, and Robert Wrigley.

Some are no longer with us, and I'd like to remember them here: Quinton Duval, Sam Hamill, Thomas Orton, Lucia Perillo, and Joan Swift.

Special thanks to Pat Solon, who's been my primary source for details about Madeline's history and convent life, and to Thomas Aslin, who helped me appreciate the finer points of her craft. Thanks also to Susan Rich, whose ideas and expertise have fueled every celebration of Madeline's work.

Many thanks to all my writing friends, especially Katie Humes, Kathleen Flenniken, Kelly Kinney Fine and Waverly Fitzgerald, for talking me through many decisions and reading my drafts.

I'm especially indebted to my parents, who have always encouraged me to do the work that matters, and to my husband Tim and our children Sarah and Tyler, for their patience with Madeline's archive boxes which were part of the furniture for over a decade. We're all grateful to the University of Massachusetts, Amherst, Libraries, for giving them a permanent home.

Finally, I'm grateful to Madeline for her long friendship and for entrusting me with her legacy. I hope this book would have made her proud.

Madeline DeFrees was born November 18, 1919, in Ontario, Oregon, and moved to Hillsboro in 1923. After graduating from St. Mary's Academy in Portland, she joined the Sisters of the Holy Names of Jesus and Mary in 1936, and was known as Sister Mary Gilbert until she reclaimed her baptismal name in 1967. She received a dispensation from her religious vows in 1973. She earned a BA in English from Marylhurst College, and an MA in Journalism from the University of Oregon.

Ms. Defrees taught at Holy Names College in Spokane, Washington, from 1950 to 1967, the University of Montana from 1967 to 1979, and the University of Massachusetts, Amherst, from 1979 to 1985, where she also directed the creative writing program. After she retired in 1985, she held residencies at Bucknell University, Eastern Washington University, and Wichita State University. She spent two years on the faculty of the Pacific University low-residency MFA program, and continued to lecture and teach around the Northwest.

Ms. DeFrees published two chapbooks and eight full-length poetry collections, including *Spectral Waves* (Copper Canyon, 2006) and *Blue Dusk: New and Selected Poems 1951-2001* (Copper Canyon, 2001), which was awarded the 2002 Lenore Marshall Poetry Prize from the Academy of American Poets. Both *Spectral Waves* and *Blue Dusk* were awarded Washington State Book Awards (2007 and 2002). Ms. DeFrees also published essays, reviews and short stories, as well as two nonfiction books about convent life. She received a Guggenheim Fellowship in Poetry and a grant from the National Endowment for the Arts. In 2008, the University of Washington awarded her the Maxine Cushing Gray Visiting Writers Fellowship.

Madeline DeFrees moved back to Portland in 2010, where she lived until her death on November 11, 2015.

Anne McDuffie writes essays, poetry, and reviews. She earned an MFA from the Rainier Writing Workshop at Pacific Lutheran University, and her awards include a 2011 Jack Straw fellowship and a 2012 Individual Artist Projects grant from 4Culture.

Anne began working with Madeline DeFrees in 2007 and was named the executor of Ms. DeFrees' literary estate after her death in 2015. She organized Ms. DeFrees' literary archive for donation to the University of Massachusetts, Amherst, Libraries, and edited two collections of her work, *Subjective Geography: A Poet's Thoughts on Life and Craft* (essays) and *Where the Horse Takes Wing: The Uncollected Poems of Madeline DeFrees*. She maintains a website dedicated to Ms. DeFrees' work at www.madelinedefrees.com.

Books by Madeline DeFrees

Poetry

Spectral Waves (2006)
Blue Dusk: New & Selected Poems (2001)
Double Dutch (1999) chapbook
Possible Sibyls (1991)
Imaginary Ancestors (1990)
The Light Station on Tillamook Rock (1990)
Magpie on the Gallows (1982)
Imaginary Ancestors (1978) chapbook
When Sky Lets Go (1978)
From the Darkroom (1964)

Prose

Subjective Geography: A Poet's Thoughts on Life and Craft, edited by
Anne McDuffie (2018)
Later Thoughts from the Springs of Silence (1962)
Springs of Silence (1953)

Publications by Two Sylvias Press:

The Daily Poet: Day-By-Day Prompts For Your Writing Practice
by Kelli Russell Agodon and Martha Silano (Print and eBook)

The Daily Poet Companion Journal (Print)

Fire On Her Tongue: An Anthology of Contemporary Women's Poetry
edited by Kelli Russell Agodon and Annette Spaulding-Convy (Print and eBook)

The Poet Tarot and Guidebook: A Deck Of Creative Exploration (Print)

Where The Horse Takes Wing: The Uncollected Poems of Madeline DeFrees
edited by Anne McDuffie (Print and eBook)

In The House Of My Father
Winner of the 2017 Two Sylvias Press Chapbook Prize
by Hiwot Adilow (Print and eBook)

Box, Winner of the 2017 Two Sylvias Press Poetry Prize
by Sue D. Burton (Print and eBook)

Tsigan: The Gypsy Poem (New Edition)
by Cecilia Woloch (Print and eBook)

PR For Poets
by Jeannine Hall Gailey (Print and eBook)

Appalachians Run Amok, Winner of the 2016 Two Sylvias Press Wilder Prize
by Adrian Blevins (Print and eBook)

Pass It On!
by Gloria J. McEwen Burgess (Print)

Killing Marias
by Claudia Castro Luna (Print and eBook)

The Ego and the Empiricist, Finalist 2016 Two Sylvias Press Chapbook Prize
by Derek Mong (Print and eBook)

The Authenticity Experiment
by Kate Carroll de Gutes (Print and eBook)

Mytheria, Finalist 2015 Two Sylvias Press Wilder Prize
by Molly Tenenbaum (Print and eBook)

Arab in Newsland , Winner of the 2016 Two Sylvias Press Chapbook Prize
by Lena Khalaf Tuffaha (Print and eBook)

The Blue Black Wet of Wood, Winner of the 2015 Two Sylvias Press Wilder Prize
by Carmen R. Gillespie (Print and eBook)

Fire Girl: Essays on India, America, and the In-Between
by Sayantani Dasgupta (Print and eBook)

Blood Song
by Michael Schmeltzer (Print and eBook)

Naming The No-Name Woman,
Winner of the 2015 Two Sylvias Press Chapbook Prize
by Jasmine An (Print and eBook)

Community Chest
by Natalie Serber (Print)

Phantom Son: A Mother's Story of Surrender
by Sharon Estill Taylor (Print and eBook)

What The Truth Tastes Like
by Martha Silano (Print and eBook)

landscape/heartbreak
by Michelle Peñaloza (Print and eBook)

Earth, Winner of the 2014 Two Sylvias Press Chapbook Prize
by Cecilia Woloch (Print and eBook)

The Cardiologist's Daughter
by Natasha Kochicheril Moni (Print and eBook)

She Returns to the Floating World
by Jeannine Hall Gailey (Print and eBook)

Hourglass Museum
by Kelli Russell Agodon (eBook)

Cloud Pharmacy
by Susan Rich (eBook)

Dear Alzheimer's: A Caregiver's Diary & Poems
by Esther Altshul Helfgott (eBook)

Listening to Mozart: Poems of Alzheimer's
by Esther Altshul Helfgott (eBook)

Crab Creek Review 30th Anniversary Issue featuring Northwest Poets edited by Kelli Russell
Agodon and Annette Spaulding-Convy (eBook)

Please visit Two Sylvias Press (www.twosylviaspress.com) for information on purchasing our print
books, eBooks, writing tools, and for submission guidelines for our annual book prizes. Two Sylvias
Press also offers editing services and manuscript consultations. Visit us online:
www.twosylviaspress.com

CPSIA information can be obtained
at www.ICGtesting.com
Printed in the USA
FSHW011539090119
54841FS